NEVER TELL YOUR NAME

By

Josie Levy Martin

ISBN: 0 7596 5708 4

This book is printed on acid free paper.

1stBooks - rev. 3/6/02

PROLOGUE

This book was written from the safety of a bright-lit study, in a pleasant house filled with beloved objects: a delicately blown Israeli vase, an Eskimo carving of a mother and child, a hand-woven basket of Idyllwild pine cones... It was written by a woman educated at a good university, a psychologist who entered the profession probably to heal herself; a writer blessed with deep friendships, but who must court the muse.

The setting in which this story was written couldn't be more different from the locale in which it actually took place... the crude sampler stitched by awkward little fingers forty-seven years ago still hangs on the wall above my desk reminding me.

I, the author, the child now grown, know many things. I have spent long, sometimes difficult years learning, remembering, understanding this hidden child. And as a writer I know how to tell stories. It was a great temptation to tell it through these wise eyes, in this older voice, and in the adult's language as I wrote the story. I wanted to interpret, inject my wisdom, my voice of experience. I wanted to shape it to reflect my present hard-won sagacity.

The child would have none of it. She absolutely would not let me.

"You weren't there, I was. Only I can tell it."

But you were so young.

"But I did these grown-up things and I remember."

Nobody will believe a little girl could remember so well.

"But the danger... I had to remember."

People won't listen to a child.

"They will if you tell it just as it happened to me!
Please, you have to."

I don't know...

It *was* her story, not the story of the woman looking back interpreting the events. The child stubbornly insisted that it must

iii

be told as *she* saw and sensed, as she felt the danger, as she trembled in the reeds by the river, as she endured and survived.

Earlier, much before the book, I had painfully learned what it cost not to listen, to ignore the pleas of a small secret girl. In reveries, dreams, nightmares she had appeared. I had borne her voiceless tantrums, her small but violent furies. Usually, she only stopped me for brief encounters. A few terrifying times I was crippled by her powerful demands when she would not stay quietly hidden; would not go away... insisting on acknowledgment.

And so, reluctantly at first, I took her hand, listened to her voice. The child raised forth the images, dictated the words; they were hers, her mystery, her unbearable loneliness, her courage, and pluck.

Often I wanted to stop, to explain as I wrote, "Listen to me with your angry finger pointing; it was for your own good... it was because you were too small that the nun... and how could *Maman* know that you were so afraid and miserable?" And always I, the crusader, wanted to preach in huge billboard sized letters that "war is bad for children and other living things," but the child refused.

"You weren't there back then and I don't want to tell it your way," and then she'd look at me only a bit shyly, knowing full well I wouldn't... I *couldn't* say no. *"...But I need you to write it down for me... I was too little."* Then she waved me on, skipping crookedly in her skimpy ill-fitting pinafore and dusty summer sandals; and I saw it through her eyes and I obeyed.

ACKNOWLEDGMENTS

Years of encouragement preceded the writing of this book. The earliest came from Jr. High School classmates, Carol Binning and Vonceil Gann, who kept asking me to "tell it again," my first glimmer that it was a story. To Mr. James Kiskadden, a history teacher at South Gate High who, upon hearing the barest sketch of my war experiences said, "Someday you'll have to write it down." To Helen T. Heath, my Los Angeles City College English professor, for her vivid use of words, her inspiration to love and respect language and writing. To Dr. Rod Langston who insisted that I acknowledge the connection of those long-ago events with the career I chose.

To Paul Hilsdale, Eileen Paris, Dr. Michael Jospe, and Kathie Rouman, who each in his and her own way made me believe that the story counted and was "not nothing."

To Holly Prado, cherished friend and teacher, whose faith and creative insights guided me toward the book long before I was ready to write it. And to the remarkable Tuesday morning writer's workshop she leads. You listened week after week, generously giving support, suggestions, and edits, chapter by chapter through endless rewrites. Forgive me if I don't name everyone, but Linda Berg, Sissy Boyd, Barbara Crane, Toke Hoppenbrouwers, Aletheia Morgan, Jane Paulson, Sharon Toriello, Rae Wilken, and Cecilia Woloch, thank you all!

To Dr. Bruce Kupelnick, whom I had the good fortune to meet in New York at the First International Hidden Child Gathering in 1991, and whose wise encouragement helped keep me on course in the early days of this project. I thank you, wherever you are. And to Frieda Scheps Weinstein, *"ame soeur,"* whose correspondence after meeting her at this event meant so much.

To my only remaining French cousin, Robert Levy, the young Maquis in the Resistance whose *nom de guerre* was *Prosper;* you are still a hero.

And *merci beaucoup* to Martine Tujague, my French friend who first went back to Lesterps, to gather photos, maps, and who shared with me her own wartime remembrances in nearby Limoges. To Michelle Ginet VanSlyke who loved the story because it matched the accounts she grew up hearing after the War; an affirmation every writer needs.

A special debt of gratitude to friends who did early readings of the complete work, for their invaluable remarks: Renee Ward, Joan Perlof, Aljean Harmetz, Ann Marple, Libby Motika, Ingrid Tedford, Jill Singer, Kathie Newton, Geney Levin, Nita Lindquist, Louise Guiney, Zorica Ilic, and Nancy Martin, dear sister-in-law, who sadly did not live to see the book published.

To my long-time editor at the Larchmont Chronicle, Jane Gilman, for her boundless enthusiasm nudging me ever on against all odds, not to leave the manuscript lying on the shelf and get it into print.

To the inspiration of my good friends in the Los Angeles Child Survivor's group. All of you have stories that bring tears, yet you endure with hope, strength, laughter, and amazing grace.

To my gifted cover designer and friend, Kelly Adachi. Your quick Yes, of course, and wonderful graphics are invaluable.

I must also express gratitude to friends, family, people who simply kept me writing with their sustaining interest and good cheer to go all the way: Cynthia Ozick, Tim Paulson, Trudy Alexy, Diane Cornwell, Carol Bishop, Carla De Govia, John and Judy Glass, Marcia Josephy, Mary Rothschild, Collete Rawitz, Jackie and Arnold Stern, Andrei Novak, Sue Carr, Evelyn Lesch, Andrew Duguid, and Sydney Swire. To my brothers Mark Levy, and Warren B. Martin. To Rachel Reichman, Lorraine Stern, Jack Nides, Hugh Levin, Jerry Felsenthal. To Daniel Soupizet, mayor of Lesterps for the honor of proclaiming me "Premiere Citoyenne", and to my son the writer, Geoffrey Martin.

But none of it would have happened, absolutely not a word of it would ever have gone beyond the long-hand version on yellow tablets if it hadn't been for Ed, my husband/computer-guru, with his love, humor, and infinite patience got me through this long long labor. I am forever yours!

TABLE OF CONTENT

FOR MY PARENTS

Sylvain and Erna Lévy

"What is remembered of the Holocaust depends on how it is remembered, and how events are remembered depends on the texts now giving them form."   Jame E. Young

MONTBRON

The street they live on is narrow. A very tall man standing in the middle could stretch out his arms and almost touch the houses that line both sides. All the houses touch each other and all the Montbron houses are French village grey.

Some of them are very old, slightly slumped, as if they were beginning to sink into the ground. Other less ancient houses attached to them seem to hold them up like good neighbors helping an elderly resident stay in line on rations day.

Maman has made a better lunch than usual because *Madame* LeRoi who owns the *epicerie* gave them a little sack of winter beans, "...under the table," *Maman* said. Josie doesn't know what that means. Her friend, Jacqueline, who is two years older says it means, "the black market." Josie stopped herself from asking what black market meant because she didn't want Jacqueline to think she knew so little. She asked *Papa* about the black market when they were standing in line for bread with their bread coupons.

Papa quietly clamped his hand over her mouth and said, "Shhh, *Ma Petite*, we don't know anything about that." The stooped woman leaning on a gnarled stick standing just behind them, raised an eyebrow and snapped. "It is a crime to deal on the black market, *Monsieur*. People get taken away for dealing. Beware, you especially, beware!"

The child wanted to kick the old woman with the hairy mole on her cheek for talking to *Papa* in that nasty tone. *Papa* acted ever so politely.

"*Ah Oui, Madame* Dupont. I assure you we do no such thing. It is unpatriotic. These regulations are for the good of all so that none are short." *Papa* took his loaf of dark bread pushing the *centimes* across the high counter to the baker's assistant and went out more quickly than they had gone in.

"I hate her." Josie said to *Papa* once out on the little street again. *Papa* looked down at his small daughter in the dark blue jacket that was too large for her, as if surprised she was still there.

1

"*Ah non, Ma Petite.* She's as old as *Petain.* She still expects he can save us. *Petain* is the leader of the Vichy government and she follows the rules, you know. An old loyalist she is."

"She has a wicked little dog that follows me and *Maman* on the street!" The child stamped her foot angrily.

"Hmm, I bet *Maman* doesn't like that a bit. You must cross the street when that happens." Then, he helped her to pull up her grey knit stockings that were drooping below her bony knees. They hurried home.

The "under the table beans" are delicious. *Maman* has made a thick vinaigrette with little tiny garlic pieces and slices of onion in which the beans soak like tiny wet pillows.

Maman says, "Soak your bread in the juices so it won't be dry. They ran out of margarine before it was my turn."

"*Cherie,* a wonderful meal!" says *Papa.* "Your *Maman* can make feasts from next to nothing," he tells his daughter. Josie loves it when *Papa* calls *Maman* "*Cherie.*" It means there will be smiles and maybe he'll sing the Gypsy song for them.

Maman gives a shy smile and says, "Have another sardine, Sylvain. Finish the last. *La Petite* doesn't eat them." Then *Maman* gets that worried face whenever she looks at the small girl. How she wishes she could buy the foods that her child would like and would fatten her up: chocolates, *gateaux,* vanilla ice. *Papa* lifts a silvery sardine from the can about the size of his little finger, lays it on his plate and delicately cuts it in half the long way with his pocket knife. Then he lifts out the thinnest branch-like bones from the center. Josie turns away as he raises the oily little fish onto his crust of bread and into his mouth. She pinches her nose against its fishy, salty smell.

"You don't know what's good, *Ma Petite.* Sardines will make you grow." *Papa* says this about anything that she doesn't like to eat. He doesn't say it about *crème caramel,* her favorite.

There's no *crème caramel* today. "No eggs," *Maman* says briskly when the child asks about it. "Now, if we only had a little chicken of our own..." *Papa* finishes his glass of red wine and makes silly clucking chicken sounds. They all laugh.

"Ah, if it wasn't for the wine... It's the only thing they don't ration, the wine. Your *Papa*, might not make it through this war." He tousles her light wavy hair and pushes his chair back.

"Don't! My bow will come off." She reaches to straighten it.

"*Alors, madame, mademoiselle...* I must return to my work now." *Papa* is not much taller than *Maman*. When he bows deeply, the small bald spot on the top of his head shows and the child goes to pat it, but he straightens up too swiftly for her.

"Sylvain, be careful. Don't go the usual route. I've heard they are out again looking for..." *Maman*'s face has no laughter left on it, "I'm afraid, I wish you didn't have to go..."

"Nonsense, it's daylight. They haven't come through in the daytime since..." She interrupts him.

"They're here now. There've been cars and trucks seen in the Basse Ville. People of St. Catherine had their papers checked. They're holding a couple of farmers for interrogation."

"Impossible, this is Charente, *Non-Occuppé*. They're not..." His outraged voice gets louder. "The *Boches* are not supposed to show themselves around Montbron... How did you hear?"

"From Edouard. He may be blind, but things reach him fast." She lowers her voice and they talk quietly among themselves.

Edouard is one of their best friends. He canes and plaits straw seats onto chairs that people buy from all over Charente. *Maman* says he does it just by touching because he can't see. She says he can tell who stops by his shop just by the footsteps.

"They're out looking for *Maquis*, resisters... but they'll pick up Gypsies and us. You know we're always in danger," *Maman* warns.

"Of course."

Papa puts on his long brown coat against the cold wind that can be felt with its hissing snow flurries that creep between gaps and ill-fitting shutters. He kisses his little daughter on both cheeks. "Brrrr, the wind from the north. We'll have snow tonight." He puffs up his cheeks as if to blow out candles.

"Promise, you'll be careful, Sylvain," *Maman* pleads again.

"More careful than an old lady on a crutch," he teases her. "Alright, I promise." He kisses *Maman* on the forehead.

"You smell like sardines, Sylvain."

3

"You smell like violets," and he is out the door.

Maman puts on her wide blue apron to begin the dishes.

"Bring the glasses first, then the plates, then the flatware," she says to her daughter as she lifts the heavy kettle of boiling water from the stove to pour it into the enameled basin.

From the window that faces the narrow street comes a loud screeching sound, then another. Loud motors rumble as if angry. "Halt! Halt! Go no farther!" Voices are heard, a scream, another scream, running footsteps. "Stop! Stop right there!"

Maman stiffens and her eyes darken. "Don't go near the window!" She hisses, still holding the steamy kettle of water.

There are shots.

Mother and child clutch each other, becoming one. An engine roars, pauses, slowly backs up. Someone shouts, "Damned road is too narrow... can't get through." *Maman* has put arms over her child's head and presses her against her bosom so hard the child must struggle for air. There is a smell stronger than sweat. Motors rumble past and soon grow fainter. It is quiet now. *Maman* loosens her grasp saying, "The dirty dogs, they couldn't get through our narrow street..." Then with a terrible start as if her body had jumped out of itself, she shrieks, "Sylvain!"

Maman runs out the door around the corner onto the Rue Carnot. She dashes ahead toward the people clustered at the end of the narrow street that opens onto the square with the fountain. The child can't keep up. *Maman* is like a... her slip shows and strands of her auburn hair shake loose from their combs. There is something... someone lying on the ground. Josie catches a glimpse through a tall boy's widespread legs.

Maman is saying over and over, *"Non-Non-Non!"* *Maman* is wild. Josie doesn't like her *Maman* to act so impolitely. There's a man lying there, very still, sleeping maybe... His shoes are just like *Papa*'s in a black coat.

Maman screams, "Sylvain!"

Josie reaches *Maman* and pulls at her skirt. "It's not *Papa*, it's another..." She wants *Maman* to stop acting crazy and fix her slip and her hair and be herself.

4

From out of a deep doorway on the far side of the street, *Papa* steps out gesturing with his arm; "Run back, you two." He points at *Maman*; "You shouldn't have come out." *Papa* sounds very mad, not like he was at lunchtime.

"Get inside! Stay there until I come home!"

Maman's face is the color of an egg shell.

HIDING

She cannot fall asleep this November evening. The night is full of surprises and excitement, like waiting for thunder after a flash of lightning. Tonight *Maman* put her daughter to bed fully dressed except for the brown shoes which she set on the fireplace mantle, "So we won't have to hunt for them in the dark." Nor did *Maman* stay for the evening prayers and sing the Fait Do-Do lullaby. *Maman* simply said, "Go to sleep until I wake you later." When Josie asked, "Why?" *Maman* gave her one of those looks that meant, not another word, go to sleep.

Josie feels the bulkiness of her blue wool jumper, the long sleeved tricot chemise and her thick hand knitted grey socks with the red borders. It is too warm under the featherbed cover, she can't sleep. She tries to figure it out. First, there was *Monsieur* LeRoi's visit before dinner. *Monsieur* LeRoi wanted them to come home with him and stay the night at his big house on the street behind them. *Maman* and *Papa* looked at each other nervously, but said, "*Non, merci.* We cannot cause such inconvenience; it would put your family in danger as well."

It would have been such fun. Nicole LeRoi had four beautiful dolls, she could have played with them, especially the porcelain faced doll, but *Papa* would not change his mind.

"*Non, merci beaucoup.* You are very kind."

Then *Oncle Charles* had come over with a green metal box and some gold coins muttering how they weren't going to get the family's treasures. *Papa* and *Oncle Charles* buried the box downstairs in the ground of the cellar. *Papa* said, "Damned Nazis won't get their hands on this, that's for sure, even if they get us."

"What is in the box, *Papa?*" Josie had asked as she watched them scatter dirt over the hole.

"None of your business! Go, go upstairs to your mother." *Papa* was not nice about it, and when she asked again, *Maman* said, "Jewelry... it's nothing for little girls. Don't ask me questions!" And she flicked off the light that hung over the kitchen table.

"I'm almost six!" Josie protested.

"This is a black-out!"

"But how will we see?"

"If we must, we'll strike a match."

"May I do it?" *Papa* sometimes let her strike the match to light his pipe.

Maman took her on her lap and put her arms around her and said, "Not now, we'll just sit quietly until *Papa* and *Oncle Charles* are finished."

Another knock. It was Gretel Bloch, carrying a candle. She came to say goodbye. "Perhaps, we'll see each other again one day when all this is over," the older woman was almost crying. Then she turned to Josie to pinch her cheek and plant a kiss on her forehead. The child stuck her tongue out as soon as Gretel turned away. She hated it when people pinched her cheeks as if they were ripe plums.

Oncle Arthur came next into the darkened room with his old flashlight and a map full of x's and little dashes. *Papa* and *Oncle Charles* studied it in the little circle of light saying things like "By the mill or by the bridge?"

"Are you sure there'll be no *Milice* posted?" *Maman* kept asking, "How long will it take to cross that field?"

The two uncles left saying, "It's a good plan, don't change your mind."

Just after the church bell sounded eight o'clock there came knocks much louder than any visitor's. *Maman* softly clamped her hand over Josie's mouth whispering right into her ear, "Not a word *Ma Petite*, not a word." *Papa* had his arms around them both for a long, long time. They had never hugged the three of them like this; it was lovelier than anything she could think of. The knocks and two harsh voices continued a few minutes. Finally, fading footsteps told them they were safe. *Maman* was shaking.

Nothing like this had ever happened before. Most evenings *Papa* listened to the BBC broadcasts when he could get them, but often the scratchy sounds made it impossible. He would read a fairy tale to the child as *Maman* washed the dishes or darned some socks. Then there would be the bowl of warm milk and honey

7

after which the child undressed slowly in front of the stove. *Maman* would take a hot brick from the oven, wrap it in an old towel and carry it to her little bed. After exactly ten minutes on *Papa*'s silver watch, Josie went to her heated bed eagerly reaching her toes for the warm brick.

This evening is better than fairy tales. This evening is mysterious like the stories Jean Pierre told to Jacqueline when he wanted to scare her. Josie loves being a little afraid and tries to stay awake just like the grown-ups in the next room.

And then *Maman* is there shaking her to wake up and forcing her feet into the brown shoes saying, "We are leaving to go toward Marton. Sit up, come!"

"In the dark? We're going to Marton?"

"Not exactly. We're going to the woods nearby."

"And pick strawberries to bring to *Tante Meta*?"

"No, silly, you can't pick strawberries at night and it's winter." Then *Maman* puts the child's arms into a coat that is too long and heavy and itches her neck.

Papa is waiting for them by the kitchen table and stands her up on it saying, "We must walk very, very fast without a word. Promise me you'll walk as fast as you can?" Josie nods, wondering whether this would be faster than a bicycle or a horse. "And you must not talk or make any sound at all. Not one."

Maman whispers, "I don't know, Sylvain, I doubt she can do it."

"She will. She must, I'll carry her. Don't worry."

Outside, in the sharp night air, the village is perfectly still. All the lights are out, but the sky is a twinkling blanket of stars. They are alive. "*Papa*, look, that big one by the Marchat's poplar trees, over..."

"Not now, hurry, faster, yes, that's it, quick, quick."

Her parents walk in long strides down an alley. Her legs have never moved so fast. She wishes they were rushing to a fancy ball at the old chateau where there would be white horse-drawn carriages with liveried footmen and pink meringue cakes as tall as fountains, just like in her fairy-tale picture book.

At a back road they slow down as she tries to breathe. Suddenly, *Papa* pushes her down into a ditch at the side of the road. "Crouch down as low as you can," he orders. *Maman* folds herself over the child as several trucks noisily ride past on the road just above them. The ground feels cold and damp against her knees and elbows.

Long after the vehicles could no longer be heard, the child says, "There's a foot on my leg."

"I couldn't help it," *Maman* replied. "Does it hurt?"

"*Non*, your lamb fur is tickling my nose." She pinches her lips together to keep the giggles inside. High up through the thorny hedgerow bordering the roadside, the moon is a thin almond butter cookie, the kind sprinkled with nuts that *Tante Meta* had made for her fifth birthday. It rests on its side in the starlit sky. This is the most beautiful night there ever was.

Papa says in his grave voice, "We won't get away so easily next time. I don't think we can keep this up. Too hard for her." His finger points at Josie. "Come here, stand behind me and stretch out your arms." Then *Papa* carefully hoists her up on his back.

"I'm a sack of walnuts *Papa*?" They laugh and run faster than a train across a wide, wide field until they reach the woods.

After a long trek with only a bit of starlight coming through the thick trees, a low whistle tells them *Oncle Charles, Tante Pauline, Oncle Arthur,* and *Tante Meta* are nearby. *Papa* sits on a tree stump panting like an exhausted locomotive. Everyone is excited. There are hugs, handshakes, and kisses. Someone, perhaps *Tante Meta*, pushes a little sugar cube in the child's mouth. They sit together close to each other sharing their warmth and relief, trying to keep very quiet. Her mother's soft coat with the Persian lamb trim smells of violets. *Papa* does not let go of her hand. He tells her what a fine girl she is to have run so fast.

"And she didn't cry when I crushed her leg in the ditch," *Maman* adds.

"You are a patriot," *Oncle Charles* tells her from close behind. "A good little soldier." Just before she drifts off to sleep, she turns to *Papa* pulling him down near her face and asks him in his ear. "Tomorrow night, can we do it again, please!"

9

Papa murmurs to his brother, "Lucky child... she has no idea of the danger."

"At least not yet," *Maman* whispers back.

LeROI'S EPICERIE

Maman and Josie are walking along the Rue Carnot to fetch a few provisions at the *epicerie*. The sky is cold and grey. It might snow again. The child skips ahead to get away from her mother. She wants to see the town crier. He limps in his dark blue uniform and carries his bugle. After the fanfare, a few people come out of the houses that surround the little square.

They say the town-crier lost half a leg in the Great War, but that he has a wooden leg attached to the knee. Josie cannot imagine how wood and flesh could be connected. She looks down at his worn boot. *Is the foot inside real or wood?*

Now the man stands tall and erect announcing in a high pitched voice something about ration tickets, curfews, weather. The child looks around the gathering of people in the square for her friend, Jacqueline. Only Jacqueline's big brother comes out.

Maman in her grey coat takes Josie's hand when the town-crier is done and guides her across the square. They head to the shop that says *Alimentation*.

The *epicerie* doesn't have much in its bins or on the shelves. There seems to be less to buy each time they go, but it still smells good. There are whiffs of cinnamon and of dried peppermint, the fragrance of linden leaves and vinegary smells of mustard.

The shop is empty. *Madame* LeRoi comes out from the backroom smiling warmly. She is thin and tall with a flowered apron covering her dark dress. "*Bonjour, Madame* Levy. *Bonjour Ma Petite.* You are late today. *Eh, comment ca va?*"

"Not so good," *Maman* answers in her exhausted voice. "We had to flee and hide again. It's the fourth time in the middle of the night in two weeks... I'm so tired. I can't sleep even on the quiet nights that we stay home..." There are little lines around her eyes, her shoulders sag. Then, as if someone has propped her up, she straightens her back and compliments *Madame* LeRoi, "What a colorful fresh apron!"

"My seamstress made it from some old curtains. Now that we can't get any pretty fabrics, one has to improvise. It's cheery, Yes?"

11

"Yes, I need some cheering," *Maman* nods.

Another customer comes in. *Madame* LeRoi puts her finger to her lips and serves the heavy-set man. He orders a half kilo of sliced ham, but he has no ration ticket for it. He argues when she tells him she cannot sell it to him without the coupon. He walks out slamming the door angrily. He spits on the threshold as he leaves.

"These wretched *Miliciens*. They come from some other village where they've already used their rations, and think they can intimidate us into selling food without tickets. Let him find a black market where he'll pay four times as much." They resume their conversation about the danger.

"And what about hiding at the LaGarde farm again?" *Madame* asks.

"Too dangerous. They have come and searched several times since New Year's. *Monsieur* LaGarde was almost taken away when he refused to unlock the storage behind the barn. They put a pistol to his head and he still wouldn't budge, but his wife began to cry, so he gave in."

"Poor Anna, what a scare." *Madame* shuddered.

"Of course there was nobody hiding back there, just some sacks of flour, winter vegetables, a barrel of apples, and cider jugs."

"I bet the *Boches* helped themselves."

"Of course, they took everything, especially the potatoes. It's so dangerous, we don't know which way to turn," *Maman* says. *Madame* LeRoi takes a piece of nougat from a drawer and hands it to the child.

"*Voila, Ma Petite.*" She continues. "There was another shooting at St Catherine last night. They were looking for the *Maquis* who had felled the trees across the railroad tracks nearby. Two boys from Ecuras were walking along the tracks. The *Boches* just shot them in the back... 15 years old... left them lying out there to die. One of them is still alive, poor boys."

"*Mon Dieu*, pity those parents." *Maman* says under her breath.

"And nothing more has been heard about *Monsieur* DuPont since he was arrested by the *Milice*?"

"*Non.* How I hate the *Miliciens.* They are worse than the Germans. They arrested him for black market activities. All the poor man sold in his little *café* was wine, lemonade, and coffee. Hadn't been selling any food for weeks. There wasn't any to be had. Believe me, I know when there's food on the black market."

"His poor wife and with a new baby on the way. She walks around in a trance. I saw her this morning," *Maman* adds.

Madame LeRoi says quietly, "Have you decided about Lesterps... for the little one?" Josie is at the other end of the shop by the store's window out of earshot.

Maman's lip trembles, she shakes her head. "I don't know... I... we... how...?" Then she falls silent.

Madame LeRoi says gently, "You can trust this nun. She herself was sent to Lesterps because she was too active in the resistance in Angouleme. She was in real danger of being caught. The Mother Superior sent her to a safer post."

The child chews on the piece of nougat that *Madame* LeRoi gave her. Her fingers are sticky because a piece of the nougat got stuck between her teeth and she had to pull it off. She wipes them on the sleeves of her blue knitted sweater. *Maman* doesn't pay attention when she talks to *Madame* LeRoi. Adults talk forever. It is so tiresome to always have to wait. *Madame* LeRoi tells more about the nun.

"She was an excellent *directrice* in Angouleme. We had such confidence in her we sent both of our older girls to school there. She is a person of highest merit; she will do anything to oppose the enemy." *Madame* brushes a strand of fine hair away from her face.

"Does she know she can be arrested for hiding Jews... one of us?" *Maman* asks hesitantly. "In Paris some nuns were helping to hide children until they could be taken across the border to Switzerland. They were caught by the *Milice* and taken away. They may never return."

"Of course she knows, but she follows her conscience, not these grotesque laws; if only more French would be as courageous. Don't wait any longer. It will be harder if all the trains are sabotaged by the *Maquis.* You'll have no way to get to Lesterps."

"It's fifty kilometers away?"

"Yes, and it's very remote. A tiny hamlet. That's why the nun was sent there. It's nowhere near main roads nor any Germans. In good weather one can get there on a bike, but not in the winter."

Maman sighs, "I don't, I can't, it's too... she's so young."

She is close to tears. "Oh I wish there would be a miracle."

Madame LeRoi takes *Maman's* hand between her own. "Have courage. One cannot give up. The Lord looks after his children," she says gently. "Many parents like you must find safety for their little ones."

Josie stands on her tiptoes to reach the shinny brass scale. Usually *Madame* LeRoi lets her take all the brass weights from their places and rearrange them. She loves seeing them all lined up from the biggest to the tiniest. They must be gold the way they glisten. The biggest one says 1K.

"And if we... if our family doesn't survive? What becomes of her?" *Maman* is practically whispering.

"Your brothers in America? It could be arranged. My husband and I would not forget her. You can trust that we would see to it. We'd follow your instructions to the letter."

Maman thanks her and tries to smile, but the smile disappears behind the handkerchief that she puts to her nose. She presents her ration coupons and makes her purchases, half a kilo of flour, linden tea, and a small sack of macaroni.

"Boil the noodles a long time," *Madame* LeRoi reminds her. "I'm afraid they're quite old and hard. It's all we could get."

"Merci *Madame*. You are a dear good friend." *Maman* puts the things in her net sack and they say *adieu*. They walk out the door. The little shop bell gives its rusted tin sound as they shut it behind them. Little snow flurries blow into their faces. Josie begins to sing:

> *Mal'brough s'en va t'en guerre,*
> *Mironton, mironton, mirontaine...*
> *Qui sait s'il reviendra?*

"Where did you learn that song?" *Maman* asks.

"From Sebastien." She sticks her tongue out as far as she can to catch a little snowflake on the tip.

"At school?"

"*Non,*" *Why does Maman always ask where I learn things?* As if somehow *Maman* has to be a part of it. "After school. It goes..."

"Who is this Mal'brough?"

"It's just a boy going off to war."

Maman frowns. The wind blows the snow off a thick chestnut tree branch above. The cold wetness tingles the child's red cheeks.

"A boy? Just a young boy?" *Maman* asks again.

Maman and *Papa* ask her too often about things in French when they don't understand. It bothers her that she has to explain things to her parents that they should know. And she hates it that her parents have accents. *Papa* said it isn't a German accent, he says it's Alsatian. Alsatian sounds funny. She doesn't sound Alsatian, she is French. She was born in France. That's for sure.

"Can I go to Jaqueline's house?" she asks, skipping to *Maman*'s quick step.

"You were there yesterday."

"We are making paper dolls and we didn't finish."

"Oh, I suppose," *Maman* says, "Only for half an hour."

The child skips ahead singing:

> *Mal'brough s'en va t'en guerre*
> *mironton, mironton, mirontaine*
> *Qui sait s'il reviendra.*

"Who knows if he'll return." *Maman* repeats the last line of the song with a lump in her throat.

Josie turns back to wave *Au Revoir* to *Maman*.

GERMANS

Jacqueline's youngest brother, Jean Pierre, and two friends are playing on the cellar steps. They're playing war with sticks for airplanes. They're dropping rock bombs on the *Boches* who are advancing on their village.

"Get'em! Hit their tanks! Pow, got that half-track!"

He points from the top of the stone stairs down into the darkness of the cellar below. Jean Pierre makes loud popping sounds that she doesn't like. She puts her hands to her ears. His friend makes a rat-tat-tat-tat noise adding to the din.

"Bombs away! Here we come... the Allies are coming... blow the *Boches* to bits!" Jean Pierre falls over as if he'd been hit. The other boys shriek.

"We got'em! Blew up all their tanks... Look at 'em run! Pow-Pow-Pow... see those Nazis run like sheep! Quick, throw a Gammon grenade!"

"*Non,* Shoot him with my Sten gun! See them fall, blood's spurting out of that dumb *Boches'* mouth."

Josie shudders. *Boches, Nazis, Germans... the enemy.* The words are hot in her ears and make her heart pound.

The enemy, *Are we the enemy?* She often wonders. *Papa, Maman, Oncle Leo, Oncle Charles, Tante Rose, Tante Ida, Opa,* her grandfather? All of them speak German. They speak German better than they speak French, that's why she sometimes has to explain French things to them. *How can that be?*

Whenever they all go on their Sunday afternoon promenades into the countryside, they only speak German to each other. They tell stories, and jokes in German; they laugh and *Opa* sings German songs. He sings *"Die Lorelei."* It's about a beautiful maiden who sat on a high cliff above the Rhine combing her long golden hair causing shipwrecks because the sailors stared at the sight of her, and ran into the river's rocks.

Ich weiss nicht vas soll es bedeuten
Dass Ich so traurige bin
Ein marchen aus alten Zeite...

But when the family returns to the edge of Montbron just before sundown, they grow quiet and speak French again, except *Opa*, who knows only a few words. If he's still speaking loud, *Maman* hushes him up.

"Why can't *Opa* speak French right?" Josie had asked after one of their walks.

"He's old, it's harder for him to learn it." *Maman* answered.

"Why didn't he learn it before?"

"Because he lived all his life in Germany. *Papa* only got him out in 1939... enough now! We don't need to talk anymore." *Maman* said in her exasperated voice.

"But why... why do all of us... are we German?" *Maman* gets one of those confused looks on her face when she doesn't know what to say. She tells the child in a tense impatient whisper.

"We are from Alsace Lorraine. It's next to Germany. You were born in Sarreguemines. You are French."

"Is that where you and *Papa* were born?"

"*Non!* And that's the end! You are making me mad with all your questions. Little girls don't need to know everything."

"But..."

"Silence! Not another word from your mouth. I want quiet for the next half hour." Josie pressed her lips together obediently. At home she went to hide under the round table with the thin cloth draped over it. She was still confused. She didn't want to be German, nor for anyone in her family to be German.

Now Jacqueline enters the hallway where Josie is waiting. She is carrying scissors. For a moment she listens to the noise coming from the top of the cellar steps. She pretends to shoot at her brother. He throws a grenade at her, she refuses to fall down when he insists she's been hit.

17

"Let's not be with them down there." She turns away toward the kitchen. "Let's make paper dolls. All they want to do is play war... and they'll make us be the dirty Germans."

BARN

Every Sunday *Papa* and Josie walk to the bottom of the village to a large barn where the Peugot is stored. *Papa* cranks up the motor to keep the battery alive. She can't remember ever riding it, it has been in storage so long. There is no petro for civilian use.

"*Papa*, tell me where we rode when I was little," she begs.

"You and *Maman* and I came here in this car from Sarreguemines when people were evacuated from Alsace Lorraine, refugees."

"I was a baby?"

"You were not yet two years old."

"Where did I sit?"

"On *Maman*'s lap." He dusts off the dark blue hood and then the roof of the two-door coupe. "Sometimes you slept. There were so many cars on all the highways. Long, long endless lines of cars, one behind another like a chain..." He puffs on the cigarette that is trapped between his middle and forefinger.

"We were lucky, lots of people didn't have cars. They were on foot carrying their belongings on their backs or in push-carts. The old refugees couldn't keep up and sat along the road... it was terrible." He shakes his head as if to empty out the bad memory. Josie takes out her handkerchief and helps to dust a fender that she can reach.

"Careful, if your handkerchief isn't clean, it will scratch." "It's clean, *Papa*, look." He's always worried about his car, even though it just sits in the barn and never goes anywhere. *Papa* goes on with the story.

"Your bed was strapped to the roof of the Peugot. It was all we were able to bring with us, your little bed."

She had heard this story before. How *Maman* had to leave behind the good furniture, the crystal, the fine Rosenthal china. But worst of all, they had to leave the toys. How she longed for those unremembered toys. She imagined entire families of dolls, doll houses, and miniature tea sets. She imagined stuffed bears and bright orange balls. Sometimes she would see herself sitting on the floor, surrounded by the beautiful before-the-war toys.

"When I grow up, I'm going to own a toy shop with one of every kind of toy in the world, even electric trains," though she'd never seen one, she told Jaqueline one day as they looked at a picture book of <u>The NutCracker Suite</u>.

The shops in the village had no toys for sale. The only ones she had played with were toys that her friends owned.

Jacqueline, her best friend, had a set of real Limoges doll dishes that had been a gift from her godmother. They were white with tiny forget-me-nots on them. She had only been allowed to look at them because Jacqueline said you had to be at least seven years old to touch them. Instead, she was allowed to play with the painted wood blocks because they were not fragile.

Sometimes they played pick-up-sticks, and once she got more than Jacqueline who said it hadn't counted because of her hangnail which made her drop some. Jacqueline always had to be the best.

Maman cut some old tin cans for the girls to use to shape mudpies. Those were her very own and they made mudpie towers when the mud was not too wet. You could decorate the mudpies with geranium petals or clovers. Jacqueline tried to make a mudpie *croque-en-bouche*, but it fell apart. They made violet tarts with the tins instead. She loved the oozing squishy mudpie, and so did Jacqueline, but rusty tins weren't real toys.

"Tell me again about my toys in Sarreguemines," she'd insist. Hearing about them was reassuring; it made her feel that she was more like the other children. It made her feel less like a refugee. *Maman* said there had been a blonde doll with a rose velvet dress wearing white gloves, but that it had not been taken out of its box because it was fragile.

"Why didn't we bring the doll in *Papa*'s car?" She had asked *Maman* once.

"Dolls! I had to bring more important things than dolls. It was more important to bring clothes, a few pots and pans. The things we needed to live. It all happened too fast. If there had been time or enough space, I'd have packed my Rosenthal china. That's what I should have packed!" *Maman* said it in an angry tone so that the child felt it was wrong that she'd asked about the doll in the box.

Then, *Maman*'s eyes would get that faraway look as if she was leaving on a distant journey. *Maman* suffered when she recalled her own beautiful things she'd had to leave behind, but only for a few moments. Finally, she'd lift up her head, her whole face would change, lines above her eyes would deepen and she'd declare loudly, "Forget it! It's all gone. We're here, that's what counts. We mustn't feel sorry for ourselves. Let's talk about something else." Then Josie would be afraid to ask what she wanted to know most of all; why were pots and pans more important than her doll?"

Papa is still polishing the head light lamps of the blue car. He doesn't seem to remember she is there. She goes over to the rope swing that hangs from the highest rafter. It is a splendid swing. It could go the full length of the barn when *Papa* gives her a hard enough push. She wishes he would push her now so she that she could feel the scoops of air whooshing against her hair gliding upwards toward the roof. Then the dizzying fall back to the ground knowing that you wouldn't hit, but thinking you might, and the slower ascent back up in the opposite direction. She wishes with all her heart that she could "pump;" that expert stretch of the body and legs that made you swing through the dusty air of the barn on your own. Back and forth forever without needing anyone to push you.

Papa slams down the louvered hood of the car, then he sits in the driver's seat for a few minutes clutching the gleaming steering wheel. They always end with a game.

"Where are you going *Papa*?"

"To Paris."

"Can I come?"

"Of course. We'll go for a drive on the Champs d'Elysee and sit at an outdoor *café* under the chestnut trees. I will order an *aperitif*."

"And can I have a hot chocolate?"

21

"No, you will have an ice chocolate *chantilly.*" It sounded so delicious, ice chocolate chantilly, that she didn't even ask what it was.

"And *Maman*, what will she have?"

"She will have a *café Liegois* and a *Napoleon.*" He opens the car door, steps out on the dashboard and flicks the cloth once more against the curved roof of the car. "We better get back. *Maman* doesn't like it when we are late."

Holding her hand, he walks her home along the Rue de la Poste.

"Josielein, we must talk about..." a large sigh, sad and strange, as if he is in great pain.

"What *Papa*?"

"The convent school... there is a nun who will take..."

He coughs and says, "it's safer there... nobody will know in Lesterps..."

"Where is Lesterps?"

He doesn't answer. She doesn't repeat the question. They don't speak for a few minutes.

She gives his hand three quick squeezes. He squeezes back with two quick ones. It is their secret signal. Nobody else knows about it. She looks up at him and his eyes are wet. He wipes them on the back of his sleeve.

Then he asks, "What do you suppose *Maman* will serve for lunch?"

"Potato soup, No!" She makes a face. It is what they have for lunch every other day it seems.

"Ah yes, *Maman*'s Sunday potato soup *chantilly!*" He jokes.

"*Chantilly* soup?" She can't help laughing.

"Why not? It's wartime."

SECRETS

It's a snowy afternoon. Josie has been playing under the small garden table by the tall window that opens onto the narrow street of their village.

Maman has divided the long dreary room into a sitting area toward the front with the kitchen half at the end. It holds the heavy wood burning stove and a walnut armoire in which she keeps odd unmatched dishes, crocks, a few pots and tins. The front is where visitors sit. She's not allowed to play there, except under the table. They sleep in a smaller dark adjoining room.

Josie hides and plays for hours under the thin white cloth that drapes the little round table. It is her special place where her one rag doll, Gigi, with the purple yarn hair, comes to life. Under that table she and Jacqueline turn into queens, princesses, wicked step mothers, and lost children. Their favorite story is Rumplestilskin. They invent dozens of names for the queen to guess like Cowribs, Spindleshanks, Melchior, Spiderlegs. Anything is possible under the table. It is enchanted and nobody else is allowed. It's their place to tell secrets.

Jaqueline told the secret of the baby sister who died before she was born.

"She's an angel watching over us now, right now."

Josie had no such big secret as a dead sister so she had to make one up. She announced that she'd seen a stork flying overhead carrying a baby wrapped in a soft cloth in its beak on the night the Marechal's baby was born.

Jaqueline, eight, said storks didn't really bring babies, but when Josie challenged her to tell where babies did come from, Jaqueline said nothing and just stared at her a long time in her superior older way.

Josie did not know then that she was to become the keeper of a very big secret that would perhaps save her life.

23

The snow falls steadily. Her parents call her to come and sit at the long oak kitchen table where they eat and where all grown-up talk takes place.

She looks up into their faces and feels something coming that she won't want to know. Maybe *granmère* was sick again? *Maman*'s been crying. It is the first of several sad talks that follows one after the other.

"*Josielein*," *Papa* begins, using the affectionate form of her name from when she'd been much smaller.

"*Josielein*," and he put his arm around *Maman*'s trembling shoulders, "I think... it would be better... I think maybe, perhaps, perhaps you will have to go away for a while," *Papa* begins.

"To stay at *Madame* Lagarde's farm like before *Noël?*" she asks eagerly. She loved it when she and *Maman* would visit the farm with all the good food and the animals, especially their puppy dog, Mussolini.

"Non, *Ma Petite*, not the farm."

"Why not?" A long silence follows this question.

"It is not safe at the farm now, they cannot keep you there."

"Where will we go?" she asks in a choked voice.

"To a convent-school where there are other little girls like you."

"Where the nuns live behind the church on the Rue de...?

"Non, not here in Montbron, but where there are... girls and you will have many friends there."

"But I have friends here, I have Jacqueline," she interrupts. *Maman* tries to help explain, her voice sticks, caught deep down inside. Then she coughs, takes a big breath and goes on.

"It is a convent, like... where children go to school in the day and they all sleep together at night, all under the same roof. It will be fun to have so many girls living together. You will be like sisters."

"And you will be there too," Josie insists. There is another long pause in which the child holds her breath.

"*Non, cherie, Maman* and I cannot stay there. It is only for students, girls."

"Then I won't go if you aren't coming with me." And she walks away and returns to Gigi and her pretend companions under the little table and sings them to sleep. Nothing further is said.

The next morning she sees *Maman* take a stack of her freshly ironed underclothes and set them in the small buckram maroon valise that *Papa* used to take when he traveled overnight to Angouleme.

"Why are you doing that? My shirts and pants go into the bottom drawer of the dresser," she shouts at her.

"Listen *cherie,* listen..." *Maman* begins.

"Put my clothes in the drawer!" she insists and rushes at the suitcase as if to attack it. *Maman* takes the girl in her arms.

"Remember what *Papa* said Sunday about the convent where you will live?"

She shakes her head violently and struggles away. She wants to run. But *Maman* holds her hard to her shaking body and then Josie hears her sob and feels the heaving of her chest. *Maman*'s face is wet and the child knows it is true.

Why Maman, why are you sending me away? she wants to scream at her, but *Maman*'s crying stops her and she says nothing at all. Instead, Josie takes her handkerchief from her small apron pocket and wipes her eyes.

"Don't cry *Maman,* don't cry, please don't cry." *Maman*'s clutch on her loosens and the child runs away. She runs next door to the warm kitchen of *Madame* Clemenceau and plays with their new kitten, Sophie, until it grows dark.

That evening *Papa* announces cheerfully, "Josielein, you are to have a new name when you live at the convent."

"I won't be me anymore?" The terrible feeling, as if her stomach would melt into nothing and her mouth dry as flannel...

"Of course, you will still be Josie, but..."

"Then I can stay here, then I don't have to go away," she insists sharply.

The father heaves a deep sorrowful sigh. "It's all arranged, it will be best for you. It will be safer with other little girls," his voice sounds uncertain, "And it will be for just a little while until..." Again that wavering sound to his voice.

"Your new name," Maman begins, "Your new last name will be L'Or, not Levy anymore.

She mouths "L'Or" silently, remembering Rumplestilskin and the rooms full of gold that the miller's daughter had to spin for the king.

"Won't that be lovely?   Listen to it, Josie L'Or."   *Maman* pronounces it as if it were a precious gift.

"L'Or, gold?" she repeats it, disbelievingly.

"Yes,"

"I will be Josie L'Or?"   For an instant there is magic at the thought of such a special golden name.   She couldn't wait to tell Jacqueline.   Gold, like *Granmère's* long chain and locket; like the king's scepter when he married the miller's daughter.   *How jealous Jacqueline will be that my name now is L'Or.*

Then *Papa* goes on gravely, "And you must never tell your name.   Absolutely tell no one your real name.   You are no longer Josie Levy.   You are Josie L'Or," He repeats it forcefully as if this force could secure the secret.

"It is beautiful," she whispers, "And will you be *Monsieur et Madame* L'Or?" she asked.   They looked at each other helplessly.

"I don't know," *Papa* answered softly.

"But if you don't have the same last name, then I cannot be your little girl anymore?"

At this *Maman* bursts into tears, and *Papa's* eyes are watery too, and all she could think was to promise them to be a good girl and to obey, and to take the new name.   She repeats what *Papa* had said earlier.

"It will only be for a little while?"

"That's right," *Papa* answered, "You will only have to stay for a very short time."

She practices the new name under the safe circle of the front table.   "Josie L'or," *I am gold, like the hidden gold that Papa and Oncle Charles buried in the dirt floor of the cellar.*

"Josie L'Or."   It sounds so rich and grand, like the rooms full of gold spun by Rumplestilskin.   Under the table she imagines golden threads spinning from the wheel twisting around the three of them keeping them close together like they had been the night of hiding in the ditch in the fields.

The next morning when she sees *Maman*'s face, she knows that it will all happen soon. That she will go to live at Lesterps in the convent-school with her secret and her new name. That she will no longer be Josie Levy, and that these two friendly rooms won't be her home anymore.

FIRST LESSONS

The room is so cold she can see her breath. She forces out little puffs to see how long they'll last. Outside, through the small alcove's window it is snowing. Is the nun still sleeping? She gathers the dark khaki brown blanket all the way over her nose. It's prickly and smells sour like a damp dog. *Maman* would order, "Hang that blanket in the garden so the sunshine can clean it." The blankets of her own bed smelled of talcum powder and felt cloudy soft. Her nose itches from the coarse blanket fibers and the ugly smell.

Soeur St. Cybard sits up in her bed, puts her fingers to her forehead, chest, and shoulders and rises all in one quick motion. Still in her plain wool nightgown she washes her face and thin neck in the basin of water poured from a white pitcher. The child shudders at the icy water. At home *Maman* always warmed the morning wash water on the wood stove for everyone's morning toilette and sang the Wake-Up song. The child pulls herself all the way under the rough khaki blanket and tries to keep from shaking.

There is a clicking sound, not quite like teeth chattering, and the words, "our father... Mary... mother of Jesus... hail Mary," repeated over and over. The child sits up to see the nun now fully dressed in her black habit kneeling at the foot of her own bed on a tiny bench facing a cross with Jesus half-naked nailed to it. She had seen Jesus on crosses before at Sainte Sulpice and at the cemetery, *but this one has nails in his hands and feet! Why was Jesus always on the cross? Why didn't someone get him down?*

The nun holds a necklace of black beads, four very large ones with smaller ones in between and another smaller metal cross also with Jesus on it hanging from the necklace. It is an ugly necklace, not like *Maman*'s millefiori glass beads that had been given to her by *Papa* when they were engaged. *Maman* said they came from Venice and the colors were like flowers in a meadow. The nun's beads are lumps of coal clicking against the sad sing-song words "Our father... Jesus holy holy... hail Mary!" coming from the nun's white up-tilted face, mysterious and distant; the bluish lips moving as rapidly as her fingers clicking those hard beads. This went on and on as she grew colder and colder. Finally she crawls back under the khaki blanket hoping the warmth of her body will reach her icy nose.

The clicking of the beads stops. "Wake up my child. Dress yourself. Your mother said you knew how to dress yourself." She obeys pulling on the clothes she took off the night before without washing herself first. *Maman* would be very cross but the nun doesn't notice. There is a stove down the hall in the kitchen, the child walks from the alcove through the icy room and almost begins to run toward the hall.

"Where are you going, *ma petite*?" The nun's voice stops her abruptly as she looks up the dark habit, past the dangling crucifix, up the beads and into the nun's sharp grey eyes.

"To the stove in the kitchen to..." she says, knowing something is very wrong.

"But you passed the cross without kneeling... the morning sacrament, the Our Father." The voice is severe. The child just stands there shaking as much from the voice as from the cold.

"I suppose you haven't been taught." The voice is mad. "I will have to teach you. I will have to teach you everything." This time the nun says it more to herself as if she had just realized it. "*Mon Dieu!*"

"Touch your fingers, the right hand! *Non*, watch me... to your forehead where your mind lives. Your breast, that's too low, not your stomach. Now your shoulders. No, no, not with both hands." The nun walked over and firmly took the child's right arm and showed her the correct order. She moves her through the motions four or five times. The child's arm feels loose and no longer her own. The nun's long fingers on her hand are dry and rough. The nails on the large hand are clipped like a man's.

"Now, go ahead, try it by yourself. Forehead, breast, left shoulder, left shoulder!" She shouts. "*A gauche*, do you not know left from right?" The nun seems annoyed with her.

"Well, I shall certainly have my hands full. May God grant me patience." Now the nun crosses herself and closes her eyes with that same look she'd had by the bed. The child stares.

29

"Children do not stare!" Her voice rises. "You must not look so directly into my eyes. Obedient children always lower their eyes when an adult speaks to them. Has nobody ever explained this to you before?" The nun shook her head, the coif bobbed and almost came undone.

The child blinks, but continues to stare up into the nun's disapproving face uncomprehending.

"Lower your eyes." She commands. The child stands paralyzed, no more able to comply than to move toward the warm kitchen stove down the hall. "When I speak to you," she grasps the small chin in her large dry hand and pushes it down slowly toward the child's blue wool jumper. "This is how you must hold your head when I or any adult addresses you. Good children do not stare into the eyes of a grown-up. It is not humble. It is disrespectful. Your eyes must be lowered to show you are ever prepared to take orders, that you are obedient and docile to Jesus Christ our Lord. Do you understand?"

The child understands nothing, but she feels her chin push into her chest and her eyes fill with stinging tears.

"Now, let me see you cross yourself without looking up." The nun demanded.

Slowly, the child begins: forehead, breast, then panic! She forgot right from left. "*Gauche, gauche,*" the nun commands. "The other arm, the arm with your bracelet." The child stares at the little silver chain on her left arm that *Maman* had given her on her last birthday. "*Oui,* good, that's your left, now the right." The child raises her head and stares up at the nun to see her approval as well as to hear it.

"Not that way! Lower your eyes. The eyes are always to the floor when we speak. Do you understand? Do it again, show me how you are to pass by the cross" The nun was trying to be patient, was trying not to shout, was trying not to think of all the duties she had before her that morning.

Tears fall from the child's eyes as they lower and stare at the faded red linoleum floor and the thin arm finally follows the right sequence. The nun is so pleased she does not notice the tears. She gives a quick pat to the child's head and rushes down the dark hall to her study.

Soeur St. Cybard must write that note for the man who will be in contact with Pierre Chaillet, the Jesuit priest who has been working to rescue Jewish children from the internment camps in the occupied zone. He and his followers promise, bribe, and trick the authorities to get the children out and then hide them. How she wishes she could be more a part of that clandestine effort, but the superior of her diocese would not permit her to join such dangerous activities.

So they sent me to this distant village where I'm to keep out of the way... She tries not to feel the resentment that swells under her stiffly starched collar. She doubts that Madeleine Barot, the secretary of CIMADE, has any restrictions placed on her. She and *L'Abbé* Glasberg from *Les Amitiés Chrétiènes* had gained entry to the Venissieux internment camp near Lyon and convinced the French officials it would be in their own interest not to be troubled with frightened, crying children. When it was time to board the trains to the labor camps, there came the miraculous announcement: The children will not leave! All of the children under the age of 16 were saved that time.

And now God has sent me one child whom I may save from the evil of that madness, she tells herself. She utters a few words of prayer giving thanks to be allowed to do something, and begins to write the note to Pierre Chaillet.

31

MORE LESONS

All alone, the child wipes her eyes on her sleeve and walks toward an open door. She hears voices, especially one that is loud and impatient, like someone about ready to scold. It is *Mademoiselle* Gilberte's, the young teacher who sat with her at dinner the night of her arrival.

"This child that will be living here, five or six, I forgot. She's so small, looks about four. Soeur St. Cybard has taken her in to fatten her up. Her people live in Angouleme or Poitiers..."

"I don't blame parents who send their children to live in the country," the cook says, picking up a pot of hot water from the stove to pour it into the basin in the sink. "There's hardly anything to eat in the cities. People are starving. Paris is the worst off, I hear. Our country air is better too." *Mademoiselle* Gilberte shrugs her shoulders as she bites into a thick slice of *pain de mie.*

The cook goes on, "Me, I'd take my cousin's girl from St. Etien, she's only seven, but not their boy who's already twelve. He's a handful, that boy is. Besides, he doesn't want to live in a small village like Lesterps and be a country bumpkin."

Mademoiselle Gilberte chews her bread slowly and says, *"Alors,* wait till you see her. Scrawny, skinny kid... looks like she's about to cry if you blink at her wrong. Be more work for us, you can be sure."

"Wonder if she wets the bed," the cook says. "Now, that would be more work."

"She's not sharing my room. I told Soeur St. Cybard right off. I said she could sleep in the little room off the washroom. *'Mais non,'* Soeur St. Cybard says that's too far away, she might get scared."

"Soeur St. Cybard is awful good about children, a real saint of a nun, not like some I've worked for," the cook adds.

"Well fine, because the child's sleeping on a cot in the alcove off her room till she gets used to being here," says *Mademoiselle* as she turns around and notices the child standing timidly in the hallway.

"Here, over here, come take your breakfast and make it quick." *Mademoiselle* calls out to her. The child enters the square room with an old stone sink and a stove that looks as if many soups have boiled over on it. Above the table hangs a medium sized cross with Jesus staring down mournfully. There's a black iron pot on the stove. It smells like porridge and disinfectant.

Mademoiselle points to a stool which she is to sit on at the end of the table. The stool is too high. As she tries to climb on it, she knocks it over making a terrible crash on the tile floor.

"*Mon Dieu!*" the cook mutters as *Mademoiselle* snaps:

"Dummy, that's too high. Take the chair. No, not my chair, the other one." This chair with the straw seat has one leg shorter than the other. It tips when she sits on it. The straw plaiting of the seat is coming apart near the center. One sharp fiber comes sticking through her wool jumper and into her bottom.

"*Voila*, your *café au lait.*" The cook sets it down before her and then puts a hot bowl of porridge next to it.

Mademoiselle Gilberte orders, "Say your prayers before you eat." The child has no idea of what she is supposed to say, and she knows she cannot ask *Mademoiselle.* Silently she crosses herself as she learned to do just a few minutes ago. That seems to satisfy *Mademoiselle.*

"Now, eat quickly, we haven't got time. I must get to the classroom to light the fire before they arrive. Don't stare, lower your eyes."

The child stares at the grey porridge. She doesn't want it. She takes the wide cup of *café au lait* in both hands and sips slowly. It's not coffee, it's chicory. *Maman* would have made tea rather than this *ersatz*, which is what *Papa* called it. She picks up the spoon for the porridge. She traces a round path in the porridge once, twice, three times. She cannot bring it to her mouth. It smells like hot glue.

"What's the matter, you don't like it?" *Mademoiselle* asks. The child looks longingly at the *pain de mie* that is sitting on a cutting board in the middle of the table with a pot of honey next to it. *Mademoiselle* slices a piece for herself, dips it in the *café au lait.* The child just sits. The cook comes over and spoons out a golden strand of honey right into the middle of the porridge path.

"There now, that should make it better." She smiles at the child revealing a missing front tooth. The child takes a dollop of honey onto her spoon, then closes her eyes and licks it slowly; then another and another. Only once does she taste the awful porridge. Four licks and the honey is no more.

Mademoiselle Gilberte says, "*Eh bien,* already you spoil her. She'll think honey is to be her daily fare."

The cook lifts a heavy cover off the top of the stove and stokes the wood with a long spoon. "Too much smoke. It needs more air." She kneels down in front to open a little iron door, flames appear. "*Ah Voila,* burn you devil, why do you make my life so hard?"

"Where are the other little girls?" asks the child. *Mademoiselle* looks annoyed. "*Papa* said there are lots."

"What is she talking about? There are no other little girls." The cook keeps poking at the wood.

"Come now," *Mademoiselle* signals toward the hall. "We must get to the classroom."

They cross an open yard enclosed on three sides by the convent building. At one end there is an iron fence with *fleur de lis* topping each spike. It's snowing lightly. A small nut tree stands in the middle of the yard no taller than *Mademoiselle*. It's thick leafless branches are iced with snow. The poor little tree all alone in the cold, the child thinks as they cross to the opposite end.

Mademoiselle opens the wide door to the cold classroom. The room looks familiar, like her classroom in Montbron at the *École Maternelle* with its rows of desks and blackboard. Only there is a thick cross at the front above the teacher's desk and a picture of a sad-faced woman under it with a golden circle above her blue hood.

Mademoiselle hands her a short broom, saying, "Sweep up the ashes around the stove, then bring up the kindling from the wood crib at the back."

Once the fire is lit in the pot belly stove, girls of all ages start arriving. They are bigger and older. They remove heavy coats, wool mufflers, hats, mittens. All are wearing brown jumpers over beige sweaters. She is the only one without a uniform. Now she feels even stranger. They look at her curiously. One tall girl smiles and tells her friend, "Oh, she's cute... resembles my little cousin in Limoges."

Mademoiselle looks up severely from her desk and says loudly "Silence," then fixes her bright blue eyes on the class until they are all seated quietly. Not another word is heard.

After prayers and roll call *Mademoiselle* Gilberte tells the class. "The girl over there is named Josie L'Or. Turn to your readers, page fifty-one. Who wants to read?"

The child hears her beautiful name spoken publicly for the first time and gulps at the strange sound of it. At least this part is like *Papa* said, she has the beautiful name.

CROSSES

Crosses. There are crosses everywhere. Every room in the convent has a cross, and there is one over every bed. There's a cross over the firewood box, over the nun's mahogany desk, over the door to the chapel. There are crosses in the library and a thin one hangs around *Mademoiselle* Gilberte's neck. A huge heavy Calvary cross stands in the middle of the cloister garden and the nun's long fingers are nearly always clutching the metal cross of her rosary. Each day begins with making the sign of the cross on bended knee.

Some of the crosses have Christ's twisted body nailed to them, those are the ones the child likes best. She stares and stares at the long bare body of Jesus. One cross shows Christ as almost a boy, but another makes him look like an old man, a beggar. Inside the chapel she counts enough crosses for all the fingers on both hands. Stone crosses, metal crosses, wooden crosses, a pale ivory cross that gleams in a shadowy corner of the chapel. The cook wears a cross covered with tiny red stones that look like rubies, but they are just garnets, Cook explained.

Over the altar in the chapel stands a large life-size cross with Jesus looking so real she can feel the nails puncturing his palms. His mother looks on helplessly. She has the saddest face in the world. *Why didn't she put the big cross flat so he would lie more comfortably? Why didn't she get him down? Why was he nailed to the cross?* In catechism class she heard Christ had to die for our sins.

She knew about sins. Sins were when you told a lie. *Maman* said it was a sin to lie. *Maman* had said, "I can tell when you lie to me by looking at your forehead. It's written in big letters so I can read it."

"I don't see it in the mirror," she had protested to *Maman*.

"Only mothers can read it," she'd replied mysteriously.

How long ago was that? She tries, but she can't remember. She only knows it has been a long time that she's been here at the convent, days, maybe weeks; a long, long grey time.

Now she has learned about crosses. Every room must have a cross for protection, to guard all from sin, to remind us of the sacraments, seven sacraments. She has memorized the seven sacraments. They are words she doesn't understand, but that she will never forget. Baptism, confirmation, eucharist, penance, extreme unction, holy orders, marriage. Marriage means long white dresses and brides and lilies of the valley. It is the only word that means something. The last sacrament is to anoint the sick.

She is sick. Sick with longing for her mother, for her father, for the too-small cozy bed with the cloud blanket, for the morning hot water, and for her chocolate cup with the dancing bears circling around the edge. The nun has scolded her for eating so little.

"I cannot have a sick child, you must eat, *ma petite*," she told her over the bean soup at supper when the child stopped after the third bite.

And now there is something else. She is afraid for her parents who live in a home where there is not a single cross to protect them. *How can Jesus protect them if he is not there? Why are there no crosses in her parents' home? How could they not know something so important? Why does Maman speak of God, but never of Jesus, his son, who died for us all on the cross?*

For several nights on the cot she has wondered how to get a cross for *Maman* and *Papa*. One could not buy one in a shop the way one could walk into a bakery and get a *pain de mie*. What sort of a store would sell crosses? Perhaps the nun would let her take the small flat cross hanging behind the woodpile. Surely, the woodpile could do without Christ's protection, but she didn't dare ask.

Each day that went by her fear for her parents grew worse. There had to be a way to get a cross to them.

And then there was still another worry. Her parents might not want a cross. Somehow when she imagines telling *Maman*, "Every home must have at least one cross on the wall so that Jesus can be welcome." She is sure *Maman* would not like it. Without knowing why, she knows *Maman* would not listen to this talk about crosses.

She remembers her mother's disapproval last summer when she begged to walk into the village church, "...just to see the rose window." Jaqueline said it had a blue in it that was bluer than a mountain lake... bluer than the delphiniums that grow along the church yard wall.

Maman had tersely replied, "Well, look at it from out here. That's enough."

"But Jaqueline says you have to see it from the inside. The sun has to be behind it." She had argued. Her mother had gotten angry.

"I've told you, we do not go into church. Church is not for us. If you disobey me I shall have to give you a good spanking." "But I want to see the baby Jesus in the mother's arms," the child begged.

Her mother interrupted loudly. "I, we do not believe in Jesus. Jesus is the Christian's God. We don't follow him. We are not Christians." She said it as if it was bad to be Christian.

"What are we then?" The child demanded an answer.

"We are... we are... we are a different religion." Here *Maman* bit her lip and looked helpless and miserable.

"What is it that we are?"

"Stop it! Stop asking me things you don't need to know. It is nothing for little girls. It is wrong to ask so many questions, you are wearing me out." *Maman* spoke in her final voice that meant not another word.

At the *Ecole Maternelle* in Montbron, at the beginning of school, the teacher's assistant had asked for all "good little Christians" to stand. She and Luciene Block were the only ones who stayed in their chairs.

"Well, what are you?" the assistant asked as if it was a great wrong not to stand.

"I am... I am... refugee!" the child spoke back. The aide rolled her eyes and the teacher smiled.

But now, sitting in the chapel, she prays to find a way to hang a cross at home in Montbron. They have to have Jesus' protection. Day after day she grows more anxious and fearful for their safety.

In the library cupboard she finds scissors and the top of an old box in the coat closet. Carefully using a book for a straight edge, she draws the outline of a cross inside the box lid. It is hard for her thin fingers to cut through the stiff cardboard.

The cross is bent and a little lopsided, but she is sure it will protect her parents from the Germans, from the Nazis, from the War. It will keep the bombs from falling on their house. The cardboard cross will keep them safe. Since it is only made of paper, *Maman* will allow it. She feels great comfort at the thought of it in her parent's house. She thanks Jesus for helping her by bending down and making the sign of the cross.

She does not try to draw Jesus on the front of the cross. She is not good at drawing people and her short pencil had no eraser left in the little steel cap. *Maman* would probably like the cross better without Jesus on it. She holds the outline carefully by the edges, then flattens it under a large book. At the right time she will ask the nun to mail the cross along with her weekly letter to her parents. She asks Jesus to begin protecting her parents right away.

"Please Jesus," she prays nightly. "Watch over *Maman* and *Papa* and keep away the *Boches* and the bombs... they are not Christians. When I come home I promise I will tell them all about you."

TARTINES

At home her bed was too small. She had definitely outgrown the small bed, but it was wartime, so no bigger bed took its place. Despite the food rationing and the war she had grown, and *Maman* was glad even though the bed didn't fit anymore.

It was in that too short bed that she had the dream of *tartines* the first time. The dream in which she stands in the long room that served as kitchen, washroom, and salon, on Rue Carnot. She holds a huge slice of bread with an icing of butter so thick she could have sunk her whole nail into it. The slice of bread is bigger than her arm, she has trouble holding it, its weight tips it past her elbow so that she can barely balance it to take a bite. When she finally has it near enough to bring her mouth to it, she wakes up.

She lay in the dark room, her parents sleeping nearby making adult sleep-sounds: a snore, a sigh, queer little moans; and she knew there would only be dark butter-less slices of bread for the *petit-dejeuner* in the morning. Her mouth was moist with the remembrance of butter and its pale, cold creaminess. There used to be buttered bread, *tartines*, every morning, but now only when the family spends a few days at the farm with *Madame* LaGarde who helps hide them from the Nazis.

At the farm there was enough food for everyone and *Maman* didn't wait until all were done before she started to eat. A large kettle hung over the open fire filled with something rich and meaty in the big kitchen. On the farm there was always snack-time in the afternoon, when round slices of bread were spread with butter from a brown crock and green goose-berry jam, and she could have a second one if she wanted it.

Madame LaGarde and her husband Pierre had no children. They offered to keep the child, saying to her parents that it was no longer safe to stay in the village with the *Boches* sweeping through looking for Jewish refugees. The child stayed with them for a week, but then her parents took her back because one night some soldiers drove up to the farm to search for the underground French resisters, the *Maquis*.

Now she has the dream again in the alcove off the room in which the nun sleeps. She is about to sink her small teeth into the paddle sized *tartines* but she wakes up! There is not the comforting sound of her parents' sleeping. What she remembers feels worse than a bad dream... her parents have left her! When the war is over, Soeur St. Cybard will arrange for the child to be sent to America, "...should the worst happen."

Papa has written letters with the names of *Maman*'s brothers and their addresses in America. The child watched the nun take the letters and lock them in a deep desk drawer along with a roll of franc notes to pay for her keep, "...should the worst happen."

In the moonlight the room looks more like a cell with its small deep set windows. The nun snores. Her black habit lies over a ladder-back chair, the large coif headpiece sits on a table like a large bird about to take flight in the air. There is also a skin-colored corset on the seat of the chair with the laces so loose that half of the corset hangs over the edge trailing the floor.

The child always pretends to be asleep when Soeur St. Cybard readies for bed, but sometimes she can't help peeking at the slow and stately undressing of the tall figure. The first time she saw the nun without her headpiece, with her patch of gray hair matted down like old straw that had been trampled, she shuddered. She hadn't quite understood nuns to be people. Nuns seemed more like dark angels with hairless cut-out faces. You couldn't tell if they were young or old.

Nuns walked silently along the narrow streets of Montbron going up the steps of the church Sainte Sulpice, or helped elderly people across the lawn of the sanitarium by the cemetery. She'd never dared look at one in the face for fear she might put a spell on her like the evil fairy in Sleeping Beauty.

Now this white bony creature... was this the same person who went about in her dignified habit and taught catechism to the day-students? The transformation to this ghost in the loose shapeless night shirt... the child doesn't dare peek again and keeps her eyes tightly shut.

The *tartines* dream is like a trick. In the convent there is no butter and there is even less food than at home where *Maman* often prepared something special for "*ma petite.*" An egg, a bit of goat cheese, boiled rice with a dusting of cinnamon. Sometimes *Maman* was annoyed when the child didn't finish these precious treats.

"But we don't have any butter," she'd say in the same sad voice as she used to remember the Rosenthal dishes when the child whined about no *tartines*. "No, not even at Sainte Catherine."

Opa, her grandfather, would walk the nine kilometers to Sainte Catherine, a tiny hamlet, to bring back whatever he could buy from a farm wife who occasionally sold him an egg, a half liter of milk, a few grams of butter. By the winter of 1943 there was no more extra food. All he came back with were some winter apples and his pockets full of walnuts that he gathered from the free fall along tree-lined lanes. *Maman* praised him and was relieved to have her nut basket full. They could make meals of black bread and walnuts, she'd announce.

At the convent day-school, Janine, a farm-girl, always has *tartines* in her lunch. Janine eats them as if they were nothing special and the child tries to sit next to her at the crowded lunch table hoping she'll offer to share her *tartines*. She never does, but sometimes she doesn't finish them and leaves behind small buttery crusts on the table. Before anyone else sees them, the girl snatches them into her mouth and for a delicious moment imagines she is with *Maman* and *Madame* LaGarde on the farm.

She is the only child living at the convent because it is war time and the boarders have all left to be with their families. At the convent she hardly eats anything, though Soeur St. Cybard raises her eyebrows so that they nearly touch the upper rim of her stiff, white coif and tells her she is a bad girl to leave food that other poor little children would be glad to eat. The child tries to take a bite of the mealy potato, but it won't go down. The nun shrugs disapprovingly, closes her slate grey eyes briefly, then goes on with her own supper. The child is glad when the nun returns to the silence she practices for hours at a time.

The child wishes herself back home eating the huge *tartine* that she dreams about. She has been told that she must always be brave and not cry and that she must never tell her real name or ask any questions. She has promised *Maman* and *Papa.*

LESTERPS

It has been over a month. It is not as cold as it was when she first came to the convent. The snowmen that the girls had made in the school yard are no longer recognizable. Their heads have spilled over and their charcoal eyes lie buried in the slush and mud that used to be snow. The ice has melted from the bare branches of the little nut tree. Each day the child looks for signs of sprouting leaves on it. The days last longer.

This afternoon there is no school. Soeur St. Cybard takes the child with her into the village on her round of errands. The child likes to come along for she has learned that the nun is very important to the people of the village. It makes the child proud to be allowed to accompany her.

First they stop at the little stone church with the squat tower and steeple up the road from the convent. Father Gregoire, the *curée*, is dusting a statue of Mary and Jesus by the harmonium. He is coughing hard. Soeur St. Cybard speaks to him as if he were an altar boy.

"You are not to be here today. You must take to your bed Father or you'll surely get the croup. Hortense promised she wouldn't let you out." She takes the frail old man's arm and leads him away. The *curée* barely protests through his coughing spasms. Sometimes he turns so red from the hacking that his bald head becomes pink. He can hardly climb the five stone steps to the parsonage.

"Come, take his other hand," the nun instructs the child. "We must get him to the door." The child shyly takes his left hand. It feels as if it might break if it were squeezed too hard. A young woman in a large blue apron comes to the door.

"Hortense, you are not looking after Father Gregoire properly. He should not have been allowed out. He is still sick." The nun says accusingly. "I think he has fever, put him straight to bed." Hortense looks abject.

"*Mais oui, mais oui,* but he would not listen to me this morning. I said, 'you are sick.' He would not listen."

"*Alors*, make him a strong cup of *tilleul*, and put some cognac in it. He must sweat it off." The old man pulls away from them and goes into the house. Hortense is agitated.

"Last night I tried to put a plaster on his chest, a special ointment from Lourdes, but he would not permit me. *Mon Dieu*, what can I do with such a man?"

"You can make him the tea with the cognac and I will fetch Doctor Blanchard. You're to take better care of him." The nun says severely.

The child follows the nun's quick walk down the lane behind the church to *Madame* Boulli's small cottage next to a chicken yard. The chickens squawk loudly as they walk by. It smells terrible.

"May I go see the rabbits?" The child asks, remembering the last visit when she was allowed to hold a small brown bunny that had been born only a week before.

"Not today," snaps the nun. "*Madame* Boulli has some bad news about her son. She will not bother with rabbits."

Madame Boulli is in tears when they come into the large room divided by a ragged curtain. "*Pauvre Raymond, mon pauvre petit* Raymond... is... missing," she weeps.

"*Alors, Madame* Boulli, let us pray for your son. Dry your eyes." *Madame* Boulli takes out a large dirty handkerchief from her stripped apron. It looks as if she has been crying in it all day. She covers her face as Soeur St. Cybard begins to recite, "Our father..." Then there are a few moments of silence. The child bows down her head inhaling a rich smell of something cooking in the large fireplace. A black iron pot hangs from a hook over the fire from which the delicious aroma escapes. It smells like *Maman*'s *cassoulet* of beans, sausages, and tomatoes. Is it possible that this plain farm woman with the red eyes and the black mole on her chin knows how to make *Maman*'s *cassoulet*?

Soeur St. Cybard commands *Madame* Boulli, "Now, let me read the letter that you received. She pulls a thin sheet of paper from a long brown envelope. She reads it silently to herself, frowns under the white band of her coif. "It says your son has been taken prisoner and is being held in Epinal, Alsace. He is NOT missing." *Madame* Boulli is overcome.

"Dear God, oh God, Raymond is not dead? He is not missing? He is alive!" She falls to her knees and puts her hands together in prayer. "Lord, oh dear Lord, *merci, merci.*"

The nun says a bit reproachfully, "When a letter arrives, you must wait. You must not invent stories. You must compose yourself and remain calm until someone can read the letter to you."

"But I could see it came from the army and it wasn't a telegram. I thought..." Now she looks embarrassed.

"*Alors,* your son is alive. I shall write a letter in your name to his commander. Perhaps there is a way for you to contact Raymond, to send food packages to the prisoner's camp."

"*Oui, oui, Madame* Boulli dashes across the room in her felt slippers and opens a cupboard. "I have a ham and these cans of potted meat. I will bake his favorite spice cake... and these bars of chocolate. I have been saving them since before he left.

They come from Belgium."

Chocolate! The child stares at three large bars of chocolate. Real chocolate, just like the bar *Maman* had saved so long at home. Chocolate was the best taste in the whole world. It takes her breath away to see so much chocolate. She remembers the piece of chocolate *Tante Meta* gave her before she left Montbron. It was wrapped in a gold paper. It was dark on the outside and there had been a cream inside that tasted of liqueur and in the middle was a cherry! *Tante Meta* told her she had bought the gold wrapped bonbon in Paris in 1940 and that this was the last one. It was a going-away gift.

"*Voici, ma petite,*" *Madame* Boulli takes down a tin and hands the child two thin biscuits. The child holds them by the edges and looks up at the nun who nods.

"Yes, you may have them." The child takes a tiny bite. It crumbles in her mouth with a vanilla taste. The nun suddenly grasps the child's shoulder scolding, "I am waiting... I am waiting!" The child swallows and looks up miserably at the nun's disapproving face. "You have forgotten something very important."

46

"*Merci... merci beaucoup Madame Boulli.*" Then she curtsies deeply holding out the skimpy skirt of her blue jumper and looks down at the plank floor.

Finally the nun declares, "You do remember. That's better. You may eat it now." The child continues to take tiny little bites around the edge of the vanilla biscuit to make it last as long as possible while *Madame* Boulli dictates a letter inquiring about Raymond. "I will send it when I pass the post office on my way to the Doctor's house. It will go out tonight."

"I hope so," *Madame* Boulli replied, "If the *Maquis* don't blow up the bridges to Confolens."

"You've heard?" The nun asks sharply.

"Yes, from Laurence, the blacksmith's son. He knows everything that's going on, but it's a secret of course." They say nothing further.

They leave the cottage and its aroma of *cassoulet* and the three chocolate bars.

Outside, the clouds have gathered. A shepherd leads a small flock of sheep across their path and they must wait in the muddy lane while the thick wooly animals pass with their ba-aa-aas.

"See how heavy their coats are. Soon it will be shearing time when spring comes," the nun remarks. "And there will be new lambs."

"Do the sheep get cold without their coats?" the child asks. The nun doesn't answer her as they hurry toward the *Centre de Ville* past the bakery, the grocer, city hall, and the *Monument aux Morts*. The villagers are very respectful when they pass the nun. The men tip their berets, the women nod politely. Today the nun does not stop, even when Francois the postman asks about making a delivery to the parsonage.

"Not now," the nun dismisses Francois and keeps walking. Soeur St. Cybard is important, the child thinks to herself once again. It makes her feel good, though she doesn't understand why.

They arrive at the Doctor's house. It is much nicer than any other house on the street. The shutters are brightly painted, there are flower boxes in the windows. The door knocker is a polished lion's head. They push a little button that makes a delicate musical sound inside. A maid in a black dress and a stiff white apron admits them silently.

They stand in the vestibule with its parquet floor and thick *Aubusson* rugs. There is a real palm tree in a brass pot by the wide staircase. The walls are covered with a shiny rose fabric that is the same color as the heavy draperies that border the floor to ceiling windows. The maid escorts them to the doctor's library, a room lined with cabinets containing leather-bound books.

Dr. Blanchard stands erect. He looks like he should be wearing a military uniform. *Papa* would describe him as, *"trés distingué."* He has grey hair, a long thin nose, and slender hands. "A man who has never touched an axe nor a shovel," *Papa* would say of such hands.

At a small table next to a desk sits a beautiful little girl, perhaps nine or ten years old. She has long brown curls, each twisted into a perfect spiral and a red bow pinned to one side. The barrette is gold. She wears a pure white blouse with tiny little flowers embroidered around the collar and a red pleated skirt. The girl does not look their way.

"Mireille is rewriting her composition," the doctor explains. Soeur St. Cybard directs the child to sit on a small petit-point covered stool. The nun speaks more softly than usual. She fingers her crucifix awkwardly. It is as if she is waiting for permission from the doctor to begin talking. Doctor Blanchard asks if she has heard anything from Prosper.

"Not since the last communication, Doctor," the nun replies in a solemn voice.

"*Alors,* that's no cause for alarm. They cannot show up like other people." The nun then tells the doctor about Father Gregoire's cough and fever, and her fear for the old man.

"Of course, he should have been allowed to retire. *C'est la guerre,* nothing is as it should be," the doctor replies. Soon they are discussing the war and how long before the Americans will land. "At Clermond Ferrand, the resistance seems more in charge than the Police. On my last visit..."

"Were you able to see your son?"

"*Non*, he is no longer at the university. He was conscripted by the Service *Travailleur Obligatoire*. Remember Laval's gift of forced labor to the German Occupation? He is working in a munitions factory, my son." The doctor's voice is contemptuous. The maid brings a tray with two cups of tea.

"How I detest the Vichy government! They have compromised France with their cooperation. Even in the face of such evidence as we had from Switzerland where *Monsignor Bernadini,* the *Papal nuncio,* received a memorandum describing the mass executions of thousands of Jews in Poland and Russia. Hundreds of thousands!" He repeats bitterly.

"*Non!*" The nun's eyes widen. "I've heard nothing about it. When did this memorandum appear?" she asks.

"Ha! Months and months ago," he answers. "It's incredible. Only the underground papers like '*J'Accuse'* wrote of it. Even now, nobody wants to know of such horror."

"And the Vichy government has cooperated with them all along." She sets down her cup of tea and closes her eyes.

The child tries not to stare at Mireille sitting nearby. She is so pretty. There is a bowl of cocoa only half finished by her elbow. Mireille has a pink holder containing three long pencils and a little steel sharpener of her own. At the convent they sharpen their stumps of pencils with a dull knife.

A princess... who sleeps on silken sheets... all of her clothes are new. She doesn't wear hand-me-downs. The child can't help staring as she imagines. *She eats brioches, and madeleines, and petit-fours. Every night there is a bon-bon on her pillow. Her dolls drink tea in rose porcelain cups.*

Mireille never looks up from her work. She copies her composition with a steel pen and a little ink pot full of purple ink. There is a big purple stain on her middle finger. The child feels invisible.

From the vestibule the large clock chimes the half hour and Soeur St. Cybard says it is time to go. Doctor Blanchard asks Mireille to bring over the composition for inspection.

"My daughter is only just learning to learn," he says slowly. He takes the sheet of paper from the girl, looks at it, and hands it to the nun. His thin brows frown slightly.

49

"*Alors*, it's not perfect!"

Mireille's face reddens when she hears the criticism. At this moment, the child feels sorry for Mireille. The nun inspects the paper, but says nothing. She hands the paper back to the unhappy girl who returns to the table to continue the work. Doctor Blanchard says he'll visit Father Gregoire on his evening rounds and they leave.

On their walk home, just before returning to the convent, old Jeanne hails them from across the street. *Oh please, don't let her come near*, the child says to herself, but the old woman waddles across. Under her chin hangs a skin bag with a huge ball in it. It looks like a loose stocking about to come off from her small head. The ball in the skin bag bounces grotesquely with every footfall as she lurches in their direction. Jeanne's eyes are very close together. When she turns her head, the lump slides forward right under her chin and looks as if it could choke her, but it rolls back into place as Jeanne says in a high squeaky voice, "Laurence is in the woods, Laurence..."

"Hush, Jeanne," the nun says. "Remember, you are not to say your nephew's name to anyone."

"Laur... he is very brave, my brother's boy, he is."

"Yes, my dear woman, but silence. Remember, you must not talk about him to anyone. You must promise me."

"Soeur St. Cybard is angry at Jeanne?" She asks in her squeaky voice.

"*Non*, I am not mad, my dear, but you will not talk to anyone in the village about Laurence or I shall be cross, very cross." Old Jeanne nods her head with the heavy skin sack bulging up and down; one moment it is a lump and the next it is a croquette.

The child shivers with disgust. She wishes she could look away, but she can't. *Where does it roll when she lies in bed?* The child wonders. *Does she wash it with her face every morning?* Finally Jeanne crosses the narrow street and goes on her way. The child can't get the horrible lump of flesh out of her mind even as she munches on the second biscuit from *Madame* Boulli.

FOOD

There is a loud knock at the front door. Cook says, "*Mon Dieu*! Who can it be? It sounds like..." Then she notices the child's frightened face and says nothing more.

They are finishing their evening meal of boiled turnips with carrots, bread and cheese. It is a meatless Wednesday. "Come, *ma petite*, eat a little more, you've hardly touched your plate."

Mademoiselle goes to open the door. A frantic voice asks if the Mother Superior is in. Hortense's husband, wearing his blue work clothes, red-faced with a kerchief tied around his neck, enters the kitchen.

"*Bonjour*," He bows quickly at the four. "Thank God, you're here. I regret to disturb you like this, but it is urgent. My brother in Angoulême has been arrested!" he blurts out. "You must help me." The man looks desperate.

"*Mademoiselle* Gilberte," the nun says sharply. "Will you go to check on Father Gregoire to see if he has taken his medicine and if he is resting comfortably?"

"Cook is supposed to go," *Mademoiselle* replies shaking her head.

"I believe Cook has to go in the opposite direction to look in on her own sick father tonight, isn't that right?" Cook nods uncertainly. "Gilberte, please, you'll have to go instead. You can have extra time off tomorrow afternoon." *Mademoiselle* doesn't answer, but she looks mad. She buttons up her wine red wool sweater and goes off down the back stairs. When the door slams shut, Soeur St. Cybard waits a few moments with her fingers to her lips, then asks quietly, "*Alors,* Henri, what has happened to your brother?"

"He was returning from his visit to us two days ago. As he and his wife got off the train, an economics controller stopped them and demanded that he open his valise."

"What of it? He wasn't smuggling arms, surely."

"When they saw the food my Hortense had packed, they accused him of dealing on the black market. He was carrying four

51

fresh eggs, a sausage, a pound of sugar, and a kilo of winter beans. We gave it to them so they'd have a little more to eat. The poor fellow, the shortages are so terrible in the cities, they can hardly live." Henri tells.

"Yes, it's true. I've heard that some people are so desperate they are eating pigeons. In Limoges the pigeons in the public squares have disappeared. God help us all." The nun presses her hands together in prayer and brings them to her forehead.

As she clears the table, Cook reports, "My friend in Paris wrote me they are rationed just enough to starve. Her neighbor died after eating some cat meat that was sold as rabbit, but it turned out to be a cat carrying some disease. Cats eat rats after all. Imagine!"

Henri continued, "My brother refused to hand the food over to the controller and they got into a fight so he was arrested. Now he's in jail! But it is not a crime to want to keep food for your family and bring it to your home."

The nun shook her head. "The controller probably wanted to profit and bring home a surprise for his own family. People will do anything these days. The *Boches* are requisitioning everything we need for their armies. There is nothing left for our people." Her eyes flashed with anger. Then she closed them and said, "Let me think, I don't know anyone from the Police, but I seem to remember the brother of our rector, a *Monsieur* Fragonard, he's a clerk at the *Gendarmerie*."

The child watches Soeur St. Cybard closely and thinks, *She knows everything! She is the smartest person in the whole village.* It makes her feel proud somehow.

"Ah Soeur St. Cybard... Hortense and I would be so grateful if you could do something." He covers his face with the kerchief around his neck. "I have been worried sick."

"Of course, I will write a letter to Monsignor and ask him to speak to his brother."

"Do you think he will he agree to it? Not all the clergy are sympathetic to us little people, I'm afraid," the man asked.

"Indeed, he will. *Eh bien,* he was one of the first to speak openly about the necessity to deal in the black market for survival." Soeur St. Cybard declared firmly.

"Is that so? I had no idea..." Cook said as she washed the dishes and the child dried them.

Maybe Mademoiselle will stay away a long, long time, the child hopes. She is never at ease when *Mademoiselle* is around.

"It's true. The archbishop of Toulouse, Msgr. Jules Gerard Saliege, declared we'll starve if we depend only on official food rations in the city. It's no sin to buy food on the black market in order to live," Soeur St. Cybard added.

"And what about those officials, the Vichy inspectors who grow rich controlling the black market? What of their sins?" Henri asks bitterly.

"That is between them and their confessors. Come to my study and we will begin the letter." The nun replies as they leave the kitchen.

Cook mumbles under her breath, "Gilberte was not happy to be sent to look in on the *curée*, there's sure to be trouble."

"Why did Soeur St. Cybard make her go?" The child asks.

"Big ears, *ma petite*, big ears." Cook dries her hands and says hurriedly, "I better leave, *Mademoiselle* Gilberte will be back any minute. She won't be pleasant. Stay out of her way, hear?"

NIGHT

The child walks slowly down the dark hall to the nun's room, as Cook suggested. A single candle on a wall sconce casts a small circle of light at the far end.

Where will I go? She shivers. Only the kitchen is truly warm these March nights. It's too cold to get undressed. She sits on her cot with the sour smelling blanket. Moonlight streams across the window panes above her bed and makes a bright patch on the floor.

> *"Au claire de la lune..."*
> *"Ma chandelle est morte,*
> *Je n'ai plus de feu."*

The part of the song about the candle going out so that there is no more fire seems so sad here. She learned that song at the *Ecole Maternelle* in Montbron. She had taught it to *Maman* and to Gigi, the ugly rag doll that *Tante Meta* had made for her. Gigi had purple hair because that was the only yarn *Tante Meta* could get, leftovers from a neighbor who was knitting a purple sweater. The doll's face had a dumb look that said, "I'm lost." The child didn't like Gigi much, but now she wishes Gigi were with her.

Gigi's body was heavy because it had been filled with sawdust. There hadn't been enough rags left after *Tante Meta* had filled the doll's head with the few pieces she'd managed to scavenge. The head flopped foolishly on the sawdust body. The limbs of the doll barely moved; they looked like grey sausages, especially after Gigi got left lying outdoors a few times. She wore a stripped orange dress, a pinafore.

Where is Gigi now? The child wonders. *Maman, Papa, Tante Meta, Opa?*

The child imagines them sleeping in their beds at home... *Maybe... maybe they're hiding in... hiding in the woods again.* She begins to tremble so hard that she falls back on the coarse cotton pillow.

She mustn't cry, she promised to be brave. She doesn't cry. She goes to sleep.

She dreams she stands inside the cloister behind the iron fence over-looking the meadow toward the road. Old Jeanne, the goiter lady goes past. She has purple hair... Oh, please, let her stay on her side of the fence... Old Jeanne screeches, "Poke your finger through the bars to let me feel how fat it is." The child refuses... Jeanne hisses like an old cat and vanishes. In the dream the child imitates the funny waddle... her skinny neck is heavy from the fleshy lump hanging down. Sebastian yells she got the lump from saying bad words. Bad words... stick in your throat... leap out of your mouth when you don't want them to... all those bad words rolled into a ball bobbing up and down her neck. It hurts, she can't breathe...

A loud slam of the door down the hall wakes the child up. She takes a deep gulp of air and hears voices. *Mademoiselle* must be back. The child quickly sits up, takes off her shoes, and climbs in under the covers. She pulls the sheet over her head and waits. She wishes she could fall asleep again, but now she is wide awake. She hopes Soeur St. Cybard won't notice she is wearing her clothes when she comes to bed.

The bell chimes nine times. The night stands still. After a while she peeks out from under the covers and looks into the blackness of the window on the other side of the room. Is this the side of the house where the swallows live?

Yesterday some swallows flew back and forth to the eaves of the main house building a mud nest. If a swallow builds a nest under your roof it means good luck. *Mademoiselle* Gilberte read them a story about a poor peasant who grew rich after the swallows built their nests under the rafters of his hut.

When the girls played outdoors they could hear their loud twitter as they swooped by. Their long powerful wings cut through the air taking them exactly where they aimed. "Swallows fly long, long distances to get to warm climates, thousands of kilometers," said *Mademoiselle*. *Mademoiselle* liked swallows a lot; you could tell from how she talked about them to the class.

55

The child wondered if they flew as far as Montbron. She listened to their twittering, it was not pretty like the cuckoos in the woods. You had to be very, very quiet to hear the cuckoo's call; cuckoos were scared of people and if you were noisy they'd fly away. The swallows must like people to build their nests so near and they must sleep like people at night; not a twitter could be heard.

On one of their nature walks with *Mademoiselle* Gilberte, they had seen two boys aiming their slingshots at the swallows that were building a nest under a deserted barn roof. *Mademoiselle* got furious, shrieking at the boys that it was an unnatural crime, worse than a sin to kill helpless birds. The boys had yelled bad words at her that the child did not understand and propelled little white pebbles in their direction. Then the boys had run away calling *Mademoiselle* names... *"salope, cocotte,"* laughing wildly.

On the way back Gabrielle Greuze had found a tiny white swallow egg spotted with brown and showed it all around. When she held it in her hand it was barely bigger than a marble. There had been an argument.

"Put it back, Gabrielle," Justine had scolded. "The egg won't hatch once it's been held by a human."

"Yes, it will, it's going to crack and a baby bird will fly out of it... long as I keep it warm, it's safe."

"No it's not. The mother won't go near it. She can tell you had your hands on it."

"How can she tell, Miss Know-it-all?"

"Because you smell like garlic."

The rest of the girls had laughed and Gabrielle had gotten mad and said, "The mother bird didn't want this egg. It was lying on the ground under the nest. That's where I found it."

"I bet. I bet you took it right out of the nest."

"Did not! The mother bird didn't want it so she dumped it out. So there, so I saved it."

"So?"

The child had gasped with shock. *What kind of a mother would throw its baby out of the nest?*

Now in her little cot, the child prays that the swallows will bring her luck, luck like *crème de chocolat* for breakfast... or that she could visit Mireille Blanchard's house again. *Maybe oh... a surprise visit from... Maman.* The thought makes her shake. She puts it out of her mind at once.

For the last time she strains to hear swallow sounds. The little wind ruffling the tall oak tree tops is all she can hear. A soft stillness floats above her. She falls into a deep sleep at last.

THURSDAY AFTERNOON

Lunch is delicious. Edouard, the handyman came by on Tuesday and brought ten kilos of winter beans, onions, and carrots. Cook got soup bones from the butcher and made a wonderful *potage*. Then Soeur St. Cybard surprised them with some small orange pippin apples that were given to her by the carpenter's wife for helping get the cough medicine for her sick baby.

"The poor woman thought the baby would die but for that medicine. She thinks I saved the child's life. Only God can save a life, but she insisted I accept something. She brought these apples up from her cellar where they've kept all winter. They are still very good; we'll have them with the *roquefort* that we got from the sheepherder."

"Not a bad meal," the cook chuckles and pushes more bread, the apples, and the cheese toward the child. "*Eh, ma petite?* See how she eats. All you have to have is decent food. We'll fatten her up yet."

After lunch Soeur St. Cybard says, "We will write the weekly letter to your parents later. I am pressed, this afternoon. I must go to the City Hall. There are refugees from Angouleme that I haven't... it doesn't matter," she says with a sudden impatience as *Mademoiselle* Gilberte's face turns curiously in her direction.

"Josie, you will stay with *Mademoiselle* this afternoon. *Mademoiselle* will take you for a walk along the Chemin du Moulin. Take a sack with you. There might be walnuts along the roadside that were buried under the snow. They should still be good even if their husks are rotted. Bring them home."

Mademoiselle Gilberte makes a face, a grimace, as the nun walks out to go to her study, but the child is happy at this assignment... *just like when Opa and I went walnut gathering at home.* She remembers how he made it into a game.

"*Ma petite*, you are so near the ground, you bend and pick and I'll carry the sack," and he would open the burlap bag as she dropped the green and black husks into it. Grandfather would point to the walnuts with his walking stick. "Over there, hiding

58

behind the rocks, and there, between the grass, and see the bunch in the ditch? Only your nimble legs can climb down there. Don't fall!"

When the sack was full, they would walk home triumphantly anticipating *Maman*'s delight at their great success.

The child hopes *Mademoiselle* will be in a good mood. The grimace means she doesn't want to, but she must obey the nun's orders like everyone else. *Mademoiselle*'s face is lost in thought as she folds the table napkins and puts them in the sideboard. The child carries the dishes to Cook at the sink who washes them. *Mademoiselle* Gilberte leaves the kitchen. Cook lets the child stand on the stool so she can help dry the dishes. "Off you go now, put on a warm sweater when you go on that walk. There are clouds and winter isn't done with us yet. I'm going home for a while. I'll be back for supper."

In the long hall she hears *Mademoiselle*'s clack-clack steps in her room upstairs. *She's in a big hurry today.* When Soeur St. Cybard leaves, *Mademoiselle* Gilberte comes down and tells the child. "I have an appointment this afternoon. You will wait for me in the enclosure at the back."

"All alone?"

"*Oui*, I won't be long."

"We'll take our walk when you come back?"

"No. Yes... afterwards." She shrugs and flicks her head impatiently.

Mademoiselle Gilberte is wearing her long light hair swept up high off her neck in a new style. She leaves behind a strong smell of cologne. *Will I be as pretty when I am big?* The child wonders. She touches her short hair wishing it was still long and curly. *Maman* had cut off her thick curls some time back before *Noël* because you could get lice with long hair and it was too hard to keep clean. *Maman* had promised that after the war she could have long hair again.

"Soeur St. Cybard wants you in the fresh air because you are always pale." With that *Mademoiselle* takes the child's hand and marches her down the back steps into the square enclosure containing nothing but the little nut tree. *Mademoiselle* Gilberte

59

locks the back door and lets herself out by the side gate after reminding the child, "Don't go out. Stay right here until I return. Promise me, I won't be long." The child nods.

There are walls on three sides of the square enclosure and chicken wire across the top. It used to be a chicken coop. Through the tall iron fence on the open side a wide field stretches down to the *Chemin du Moulin*, lined with tall birches. It is warm in the sunshine, but big puffy clouds scud across the sky to cover it from time to time. When the sun is covered, it's chilly. She wishes she had worn her sweater like Cook said.

She watches the clouds a long time. *What fun it must be to be an angel living among the deep and puffy clouds and fall into their round softness.* Cook has told her that every child has a guardian angel who watches over them and keeps harm away.

"Even refugee children?"

"Yes, all children, especially those."

"How old is the guardian angel?"

"Angels are ageless."

"Is mine a boy or a girl?"

"It is just an angel, God's messenger who takes your prayers straight up to God in heaven."

The child imagines angels floating back and forth between the clouds pulling in their wings so they wouldn't catch. "Please, my guardian angel," she whispers. "Make *Mademoiselle* come back so we can take our walk." The clouds keep moving, but the gate stays shut.

She walks to the little hazelnut tree, stretches, and to her surprise, she can touch the lowest branch. *I can reach it! I've never done that before... maybe, it's just a bush. No, the trunk is bigger than a bush. It's a tree and I can reach it!*

Then she skips to the iron fence and listens for the sound of footsteps, there's a crunch on the gravel path on the other side of the gate that she can't see. She waits, the sound fades. A dog barks far away. The child returns to the tree.

How alone it must be without any trees nearby, she thinks. A breeze makes the tree shiver its small oval leaves. They are new and clustered among them are tiny little buds, almost invisible.

"When did you get these leaves?" She asks the tree. "Last week your branches were bare." The tree's delicate foliage flutters again. She imagines it is nodding at her.

"I want... I want *Maman*. I want *Maman*." She hears herself say the forbidden words. The words that she wouldn't say. The words that she kept pushed way down deep in her chest for all these weeks, for all these months?

"I want *Maman* and *Papa* and my bed with the cloud cover and my cup with the dancing bears."

And then come the worst words of all... "Will I ever see *Maman* again?" She shakes so hard it hurts. The sun has disappeared.

"*Maman, Maman, Maman*, take me home!" She cries.

"*Maman, Maman* where are you?"

She cries so hard the sobs are hiccups that she can't stop. Her chest heaves in successive spasms so that she can hardly breathe between the sobs. She blows her nose into her handkerchief with the red "J" that *Maman* embroidered in the corner. She stuffs the corner into her mouth. A dog barks loudly. The sobs come more slowly now. The little tree stands absolutely still and quiet.

She stretches up both hands and curls her fingers around the branch that she can reach, lifts her feet up from the ground and sways back and forth. The tree limb bends under her weight, but it does not break. When her thin arms give out, she drops to the ground lightly. Some twigs fall down.

"This forked twig could make a sling shot," she tells the tree. "Jaqueline's brother made sling shots and shot pebbles at sparrows... and Jaqueline..." *Jaqueline, if only Jaqueline could be here now in the enclosure. We would play stoop tag. I would be IT. We would race on one foot from the house to the classroom. We would draw a hopscotch in the dirt under my little tree.*

She starts to shake again though the sun has reappeared from behind the clouds. This afternoon is forever.

DRESSES

The girls are having lunch in the refectory. The child eyes the buttered *tartines* that some of the girls unpack. *It's not fair.* Two seniors are talking about when the Allies are going to land in France and that the war will be over once they are here. Another girl calls them crazy because the *Boches* are too strong; "Nazis will win," she argues.

"When the Americans get here they'll give away chewing gum to everybody," another girls announces.

"I love the Americans," says the first.

The child turns toward Janine who is biting into her buttered *tartine.* Janine makes a face, "Ugh... it tastes funny, I don't want it. Here, you can have it."

The child takes it and stuffs a piece into her mouth. It's delicious. *How can Janine not want it?* Janine is seven and a half; she talks about the beautiful white dress that is being made for her First Communion. She talks about it all the time.

"It's just like a wedding dress and it has a veil."

"What is a veil?"

"Don't you know what a veil is?"

The child shakes her head and worries. Something else she is supposed to know. There are so many things she doesn't know since coming to the convent like about the rules of going to Heaven, Limbo, or Hell. And she doesn't understand what makes the water holy. Father Gregoire pours water into the angel basin at the door of the chapel from the same pitcher as he uses to drink. She wonders about the Host and the Body of the Lord and his blood. Now there's chewing gum and the veil.

It seems as if the others know everything important except her. Like everybody knows the Jews killed Christ but she hadn't known. It had made her uneasy. She had a terrible dream that *Papa* got sent far, far away. When she asked *Maman* why they took him, "For killing Jesus," *Maman* replied sadly. She woke up crying and the nun asked her what was the matter.

"Nothing," she said.

"A veil is to cover your face. It goes on the crown on your head, Janine gestured. You have to have it for First Communion." Janine was peeling her hard-boiled egg.

"How can you see?" the child asked timidly.

"You see through it, it's like a net." The child licked the corners of her mouth to get the last smear of butter. "My veil is going to have white carnations pinned at the top and the dress will be long with flowers on the sleeves and my sister is giving me her white gloves to wear, and the skirt will be satin and ribbon bows. I'm going to have the prettiest dress of all."

Janine popped half of the hard-boiled egg into her mouth, threw the other half into the trash, then took a long drink of cider from the bottle in her lunch basket.

"And my mother might get me white net stockings like they had before the war."

In the beginning, the child didn't pay attention to all the talk about First Communion. She hardly noticed how girls dressed. Everybody looked the same in their drab washed out jumpers and thick wool sweaters. But everyday more of the juniors told about the white dresses they were going to have for the ceremony. The child listened solemnly to the excitement that would come over them as they spoke of it. Everything had to be white, the symbol of purity. It sounded like a fairy tale, all the girls walking in a row, dressed like brides carrying golden missals. Madeline said her rosary would be real mother-of-pearl. The girls had to remember a lot of long prayers in Latin and hymns.

She wondered anxiously if she was going to be one of the girls dressed in white. Soeur St. Cybard had not talked about it. *Mademoiselle* Gilberte didn't seem to care much whether she learned the prayers at catechism or not.

Now Janine talks about the feast they will have afterwards.

"My mother promised to make *profiteroles.*" The child doesn't dare ask what these are.

"What else?"

"*Clafoutis* with cherries. There will be *Sautée de Lapin au Vin Blanc*, rabbit stewed in white wine sauce."

63

Rabbit. She had seen the long skinless animals hanging by their paws on a hook at the butcher in Montbron. They looked naked and creepy. She didn't know whether to feel sad or embarrassed to see them without their soft furry coats. She was glad *Maman* had never cooked rabbit. Sometimes it was all the butcher had, but still *Maman* wouldn't buy it. "We don't eat rabbit," she had explained simply as the butcher shrugged.

"Will there be chocolate?"

"Of course, silly, the *profiteroles* have chocolate sauce poured all over them."

The child catches her breath. *Chocolate sauce?* She has never heard of chocolate sauce, but she doesn't tell Janine.

"And who will come to the Feast?" asks the child timidly.

"All my family, even the ones from Poitiers and Cognac."

"And... classmates, Paulette, Myrtile, Monique? Do they come?"

"No, of course not. Everyone has her own feast afterwards and they go to their own."

LETTERS

"I am waiting child; I don't have all afternoon."

Soeur St. Cybard's voice comes from her study. The child knows it's time for the weekly letter home, but she doesn't like to write letters to her parents.

Can I tell Maman about Mademoiselle? Can I tell her about First Communion? She wouldn't like it... catechism class, and going to chapel every day, and the little basin with the holy water and the angel in the middle where we dip our hand before making the sign of the cross... the beautiful smell of the chapel when Father Gregoire swings the censer...

She can hear the swish of the nun's heavy habit moving quickly across the room. The child hangs her head and just stands outside the opened doorway.

"Come now, what is this great hesitation? Your *Maman* and *Papa* depend on your letters to know their little girl is well so they won't worry. Enter!" She looks down at the child reproachfully. "You've had all week to think about it," she says, as she points to the chair for her to sit in. Then she goes behind the big desk, picks up the steel pen, dips it into the purple inkwell and says aloud as she writes, "*Chere Maman et Papa.*"

After long, long silence, the child begins to dictate in a barely audible voice, as she does every week.

"I am fine, how are you? I go to school. I practice making beautiful letters... *Mademoiselle* Gilberte is teaching us to embroider with colored yarn on a sampler."

She has started the sampler and she is on her fourth row of blue x's. The second row had to be completely taken out because she had left too much space between some of the x's. *Mademoiselle* had gotten very angry and told her to take it out one by one without the scissors because yarn was too scarce. It took hours of pulling the yarn out with a blunt needle, first on one side, then the other. One of the older day-students, Maria, with much stronger fingers had helped her.

Everybody says Maria is going to be a nun. She prays more seriously and sincerely than anyone, just as saints do. "God doesn't

65

listen if you pray the words and aren't thinking hard about them at the same time," said Soeur St. Cybard at catechism class. Maria is kind to the child and doesn't tease like the other big girls. She always helps out. It was Maria who volunteered to clean the ashes out of the dirty heater.

Some of the girls mock Maria behind her back because she's so pious and never gets in trouble and always gets first place in her studies. *Why must they be so mean?* the child wonders.

"Maria's heard the call." Justine hissed under her breath. "She's always doing good deeds and stupid stuff like that. She probably has visions and hears voices like Joan of Arc or Sainte Bernadette."

Another girl added, "And she makes more sacrifices than anyone. I bet she even stings herself with nettles during Lent. I can't stand her."

The others just shrugged and looked uncomfortable and started to talk about the feast last year on Corpus Christi day, that there were cream puffs, real cream puffs.

The nun interrupts her daydreaming. "What a long, long silence. You are certainly taking your time to think. Did your brain go to sleep?"

The child strains to dictate, "*Maman*, please send me a white dress and a veil for Holy Communion." The nun's pale eyebrows go up in surprise.

"Non, *ma petite*, this will not do. You cannot have Holy Communion."

"I can't?" She doesn't understand. "All the girls..."

"I know, but it's not possible for you." Now it's her turn to become silent as she bites her lip, puts her hands together in a prayer bowing her head just above them. The child knows to keep silent when nun is in prayer, but why is she doing it now in the middle of dictation?

"I can't have...?" the child says softly.

"You have no Baptism papers. It's... before one can take communion, one must be baptized."

"But that's for babies, I'm too big."

"One is never too big to be baptized," the nun replies gently.

"Can I do it?"

The nun shakes her head sadly, "It must be with your parent's permission. First, they must allow it. We cannot, no, not without... you have to have Baptism Papers."

The child is confused. Papers, more papers. Grownups were always talking about having papers. Papers to go from here to there. Papers to stay. Papers on the train to show who you are. Papers to get rations. Papers to get coal. *Oncle Leo* got his papers, "...at the last minute to go to America." Now you have to have papers before Jesus can enter your heart and make you pure.

"Let's write to my parents to get permission so I can be baptized."

"Hmmmm, *Mon Dieu*, what to do?" The nun looks troubled.

"Perhaps this should be a short letter today so we can get it into the letterbox before the collection." She writes a few lines very rapidly the way she always does at the end of the dictation, folds the thin onion skin sheet in half, puts it in a blue envelope. After she has written on the front of the envelope, she directs the child to carry it carefully downstairs where the handyman will take it to the post office on his way home.

BABY JESUS

The Spring sun is warm; bees buzz under the little nut tree. She sits holding a picture smaller than a postcard that Janine gave her. She has been looking at it for several minutes. She can tell it's heaven by the streaks of light shining down on the angels hovering with their hands clasped together and their wings spread wide... I am an angel... see my full robes... my golden hair, I can only be an angel, they seem to be saying.

The child wonders. *Does my guardian angel look like them? Is it a boy or a girl?* Angels, you can't tell what they are by their clothes. You can't tell by their hair. In the paintings of Jesus in the chapel you couldn't tell either, except that Jesus always has a beard as well as long hair. The angels in this picture have faces just like Jesus, but none have beards. Their faces are so soft and kind; they are probably young girls. All angels look pale like they could burn easily in the sun. They look obedient, and polite too. Even in the strong light, they don't squint. They look like they wouldn't know how to be any other way.

Cook says the way God gets angels is to make babies die. When a baby dies, it happens before it can sin. Its soul is so pure that God takes it straight to heaven. In heaven the baby grows up to become a servant of God. Since it has never sinned on earth, it stays pure forever. That's why angels always have that soft kind look on their faces. Cook said her first baby boy was taken by God to be an angel.

"How old was the baby?"

"Four months; he died of the croup. He went to be with God."

"Did you want him to be with God?" The child can't imagine it.

"If God needed him, then I had to let him go." Cook answered with a sad face.

"But there are angels all over heaven, why did he need your little boy?" The child asks.

"Somebody here on earth needed an angel and so God called my little son." She replied peeling another potato.

"But, he shouldn't have taken your first one." Cook gives a smile. "Never mind, it was a long time ago that my petit Jean Claude went. I know he is safe with God and it comforts me."

In the picture, the bottom angel's robe swirls around Mary the mother, who is bending over her own baby Jesus lying on a rumpled piece of sheet with straw underneath. Jesus looks asleep though his eyes are open. His pudgy body looks just like a baby's, but the face doesn't. *It's too serious.* Maybe Jesus knew already that he was going to die on a cross. Being the son of God, he probably knew right away. *His worried mother must know too.*

The child leans against the trunk of the nut tree and stares at the spiky scales growing from the bare branches. Catkins, fuzzy clusters of yellowish, grayish, green. When they get a little longer, they will droop down and she'll be able to touch their soft furry fluff.

She looks back at the picture. On the other side of where the baby lies is Joseph. He's wearing a dark robe with a white beard and white hair. That's how God must look. Joseph is also the father of Jesus, but Jesus is the son of God. She doesn't understand. Joseph looks upset too. All three of them do.

Maybe it's because they had to stay in a barn with their baby on a bed of straw. The baby has no clothes on, but its leg is bent so that you can't see anything. The big painting of Jesus in the chapel shows him naked too, but there's that same rumpled piece of cloth tied around him so nothing shows. And there's blood on his feet and hands from the nails punched through them. *How can the nails hold up his long body just by the hands without tearing them?* The chicken wire over the coops has a lot of nails to keep it from coming off. They're rusty.

A stiff breeze comes up. The child wonders how long will it be before the hazel nuts grow on the bare catkin branches. The rust brown nuts are *Maman*'s favorite with their sweet taste. When they are ripe, she will fill a sack for *Maman* and save them until...

The baby must be cold lying there naked. Even if they are poor they should have something to keep him warm. Why doesn't

Mary take that cloth draped over her head and cover the baby with it? There's a glow of golden light all around the baby. That probably keeps him warm. A lot of the people in the chapel paintings have these golden rings around their heads. Halos. Halos mean they're saints.

Is Soeur St. Cybard a saint? She's pale like an angel and she gets that look on her face when she prays just like the angels. But when she's disappointed, her face looks like *Madame* LaGarde looked after two chickens were stolen by a fox. The child has never seen a halo around Soeur St. Cybard's head.

Now she looks up at the sun through the nut tree's branches. If she stares a few seconds, then closes her eyes, white hot halos appear inside her eyelids... they don't last long. A bell from the chapel rings the quarter hour. She grabs the lowest branch, it is small enough that she can put her hand around it, but when she pulls on it, all it does is bend. "How strong this little tree is," she says aloud.

The child stares at Jesus in the picture again. Even though he's just a baby, they're acting as if he's already more important than anyone else. So many angels protecting him must be because he's more special than other babies they're supposed to guard. She envies this baby Jesus.

"Lucky baby to have been born long ago before there were Nazis and *Boches*... and the war," she whispers. Something feels thick and dry in her throat, like a piece of dark bread that won't go down. *Papa* said to be brave. Holding back the tears is harder when the wind blows. Maybe today *Mademoiselle* won't make her stay out here by herself so long.

SHAME

Any moment, Soeur St. Cybard will call her to her study and demand that she dictate another letter.   She dreads these afternoons more each time. *Letters, why is it so hard?* She loves her parents and she loves to practice writing at school.   It must be something else.

Maybe if she hides downstairs by the kitchen... *Chere Maman cher Papa.* She doesn't know what else to say, she doesn't know what she's supposed to do.   She hasn't gotten a letter for a long time. Soeur St. Cybard says the mail can't get through because of the blockades and sabotage. *What is sabotage?* Some letters take a month to get here, even from as nearby as Confolens.

"The *Maquis* are doing their job!" says the nun, then bows her head and prays. *Why does she pray so much?*

If the child hides, the nun might not try to find her. She is always in such a hurry. She wishes she had more time. She wishes she could be with her more, instead of having to be with *Mademoiselle* Gilberte who doesn't like her. Soeur St. Cybard is very serious, but she doesn't mind having the child living here, the nun told the cook.

"*La petite...* it's nice to have little ones among us. They make us smile more." She likes to hear the child recite prayers and says she must be smart to have memorized the long ones so quickly. Sometimes she says, "You're a *bavarde,* you chatter too much, and you ask so many questions, but she doesn't get angry at the questions the way *Maman* did.

Last week the nun let her come along to chapel to ring the Angelus in the evening. The altar boy was sick and couldn't come. She let her hold one of the ropes while she yanked the pull to sound the bells in the belfry tower. At first the sound was so loud, she thought it would stay forever in her ears, but then she liked how it entered her whole body and made it shiver as if she had become the echo. For a long, long time afterwards she could feel the force of the bell's ring through her. It was a little bit the way a new song gets into your head and you keep hearing it over and

71

over until you wish you could forget it. But she liked keeping the rich deep bell sounds in her head.

Maybe she'd hide in the bell tower, climb the stairs to the top of the steeple and look down on the village. Like being an angel looking down from heaven. You can see the little bunch of houses and the farms scattered across the countryside. You can see the *Chemin du Moulin* with the poplar trees that line it all the way down to the river where *Mademoiselle* takes her on walks. The sheep look as little as dogs from up there in the steeple. Far in the distance, there is another little village.

"Come now, Josie, I'm waiting." The nun calls out.

"Let it be tomorrow, let me be invisible," she whispers. But it wouldn't be any good. Jesus would still be able to see her. Jesus sees everything, He is always there, and if we are good He enters our hearts. She cannot hide from Jesus. She walks to the study.

The nun is standing with her back to her. She faces the wall with the crucifix. She stays this way a long time. The child is used to these silences when the nun is absolutely still with her hands clasped, gone to some deep far away place. Cook says nuns practice silence. She waits as quietly as she can. Perhaps she will remain this way and there won't be a dictation; please Jesus.

Soeur St. Cybard turns back toward the desk and sits in her chair. The fluted pleats of her *cornette* seem too tight around her face. Does it itch to have a tightly starched band pressing constantly against her cheeks, the child wonders.

"In less than an hour I must meet with the mayor. Are you ready?"

She nods, but she cannot think of anything to say. This time it doesn't feel as if the words are caught in her throat. Today she has no words and she can't think. She stares out the window Rivulets of rain are streaking down the pane like little upright streams.

"*Alors,* what do you want to tell your parents?" Her voice is not quite mad, but it could get that way.

She knows she must begin. But her lips are pressed together like unopened pages. She becomes a statue; inside she's hot.

Maman, Papa, come and get me. Oh please take me home.

"So, you have nothing to say?" Grey eyes bore into her face. The child lowers hers. "Why is it the cat always gets your tongue when it's letter writing time? Well, we'll wait here until your tongue loosens."

Maman, Papa, where are you? You said only a little while.

"*Alors*, this is very bad!" Now the nun is angry. She stands behind the desk, reaches across to lift the child's chin and says, "This will not do!" Her low voice is very grave.

"Begin," she commands.

The child wants to begin, not even the *Chere Maman et Papa* come out. There is something swelling inside her throat. She can't push it through.

Then the nun begins aloud:

> "*Chere Maman et Papa.* I am a very, very bad girl. I am stubborn and disagreeable. I do not want to talk to you. I do not want to write you letters."

Her steel pen and the purple ink move across the paper like a string unwinding. The child watches her form the words and stops breathing. *Very, very bad girl!* The words sound in her ears and her cheeks grow so hot that tears melt down her face. She begins to sob. *This... is why they sent me away... bad girl...* The nun knows it too.

"No, no," she begs. "Please, no, don't!" She wants to snatch the paper from the desk and run away. *Maman...Papa...they'll never let me come home because I'm a very, very...* Strangling sounds in her throat. She wants to die.

The nun sends the child out of the study saying, "You will spend the rest of the afternoon by yourself so that you may address yourself to God and pray to be forgiven."

The child walks down the long corridor crying, past the kitchen, down the stairs, past the brooms and the woodpile to the enclosure. She stands under the little tree holding on to the trunk. *Very, very bad girl!* The words ring in her ears like the bells in the chapel. The rain comes down softly.

SHEEP

School is off for a week. It's sheep shearing time. The girls must help. All hands are needed. Every morning they walk or bicycle from the convent to the old rough wood sheds in the sheep meadows on the outskirts of the village where mountains of wool fleeces are piled in heaps. On their way they can see the freshly shorn sheep. They look much smaller than before their haircuts. Janine says they aren't cold though they look naked in the spring breeze.

The child hopes the lambs will come down the path, but most stay off in the distance. Sometimes two lambs crouch under one mother, suckling. *They always stay close to their mothers...* she notices the lambs never move far off.

The school girls' job is to pull twigs, little pebbles, sand and dead leaves from the shorn wool. It smells terrible in the shed, like stale grease, worse than wet wool smell, worse than the chicken coops after a rain. The girls pinch their noses with their fingers for as long as possible until they have to start pulling and sorting.

Even with the thick smell it's fun. The girls like this better than studying at their desks in school with *Mademoiselle* Gilberte. She doesn't stay with them, just a few herders and the team of sheep shearers who go from village to village. Here in the shed they can talk all they want to and nobody tells them to be still. The child is proud that she has been included. At first some thought she was too little to help, but when she filled her first bag of wool in no more time than it took the juniors, she was soon just one more helper.

Madame Boulli supervises the girls in one shed; an old woman with only one eye wearing wooden shoes with straw inside them is in charge of the other. The herders and their helpers come by and tease the girls good naturedly. It's lively. At lunch time everyone eats outside on large tables set up on trestles in the shade of an old chestnut tree. The sheep owner's wife brings out pots of *hachee parmentier*, a tasty hash, white beans in oil vinaigrette, fresh radishes that look like pink and white decorations, and round loaves of bread. Red wine is served and each girl is poured some water with a few drops of wine turning it into *rosé*. Afterwards there are pears and goat cheese and more crusty bread.

After lunch they walk around the farm and lie on the grass for a nap. Today the child goes with Janine to the duck pond to watch the geese.

Two young fellows who help the shearers are sitting on the fence by the rusty wheelbarrow. Their backs are to the girls.

"I delivered plastique for demolition to Prosper," says the huskier one.

"You saw Prosper?" The slender one asks incredulously.

"Yes, but not his face, it was dark. He's not tall."

"And the others?"

"There were three or four, but I couldn't tell who they were. They asked me the password and my code name... that was all."

"Did you see Laurence?"

"I don't know, he might have been one of them. They don't like to be recognized, you see."

"But Laurence is your friend."

"It's not the same once you join the Resistance. Laurence never talks to me anymore when we see each other in the village. It's better. The commander who trained us said there's no danger of giving away secrets if we don't talk. Me, I'm only telling you."

"Lucky! I'm still waiting for my assignment. I think they have forgotten all about me," the shorter one says impatiently.

"*Non,* just wait. It's dangerous, you know. Don't be in such a hurry. There was hardly any moonlight on my mission when I took my bicycle through the woods. I was sure I'd step on a landmine or some trap, and there are snakes too."

"Snakes?" The short one cries out.

"Hush, get a hold of yourself."

"I'm not scared of the *Boches*, but the snakes," he mutters.

"That's war for you. If you want to work in the underground as a *Maquis*...it's dangerous, *Voila*." The boys, seeing the girls walk toward the well, pull up a bucket and splash their faces.

"What's *Maquis*?" the child whispers to Janine.

"I don't know," Janine shrugs. "I wish we had some bread for the ducks; here they come." Six white ducks swim toward the girls on the edge of the muddy pond.

"Bread? For the ducks?"

"Of course, they like to eat it."

The child falls into silence. *Janine would give bread to the ducks?*

"Bread is... you have to save bread, Janine. It's too... bread is only for people."

"We always give stale crusts to the ducks at our farm. That's how they get fat."

The child is puzzled. Cook always saves each little piece of bread carefully in the breadbox as if it were coins. Janine's family must be very rich. That's why she always has buttered *tartines*.

They return to the work in the shed and the barn giggling and holding their noses as they enter. *Madame* Boulli points them to a new heap that has just been dumped in the middle of the floor. They pull clumps of the coarse wool from the dark ivory colored fleece.

Madame Boulli says, "This must have been a very dirty herd, I've never seen darker wool. Don't know if it'll bring much money."

Another woman who has joined them answers, "That's why we're so glad to have these girls helping. Mind, you don't cut your fingers. Some of these sheep must have rolled in nettles like the penitents. They're sticky and they burn."

The clumps of wool are oily and the burrs and seeds are hard to get out. Two of the older girls inspect the shreds of picked wool before allowing it to be stuffed in the sacks which will be graded and weighed in another shed.

"This still has sand and dirt in it," one inspector tells Janine. Take it back and do it right."

Janine makes a face and sticks her tongue out at the girl as soon as her back is turned.

"I wish they would bring us wool from the lambs, it wouldn't be filthy and smelly like this stuff. *Maman* says I don't have to do this if I don't want to."

The child doesn't understand Janine at all. She continues pulling and tugging at her own clump. It has the head of a dried wheat stalk caught in it. Every time she pulls on it, pieces crumble and must be dug out separately, but she likes doing it. It's very grown up work.

Madame Boulli's friend says in a half whisper. "*Eh*, what do you think? The Allies are going to land in France soon. My godson is sure of it. Then this war will be over. Think of that."

"I don't believe it. How does he know?"

"He listens to the BBC broadcasts."

"But that's forbidden," *Madame* Boulli says sharply.

"Doesn't stop him... and I'm glad."

Madame Boulli looks doubtful and unhappy. "Yes, I want the war to end as soon as possible, but can we count on the *Boches* to return our prisoners? My Raymond... oh, if anything worse should happen. I don't know anymore."

Janine stands up and yawns, "Let's go outside, it's too hot." she mumbles. The child keeps on pulling at the clumps.

"*Écoute, ma chère,*" *Madame* Boulli's friend replies. "There have been hardly any Germans around these parts. Those that have been by have been very correct. It's the *Milliciens* that I'm more afraid of personally. You know about the arrest they made of *Madame* Gaston. They accused her of aiding the *Maquis*. They said she provided them with food and that she allowed munition drops to be made on her property in the woods."

"I was afraid Simone Gaston would get caught. She's the bravest woman I know and the most generous." *Madame* Boulli shakes her head sadly.

"It was that bastard Xavier who betrayed her; I'm sure of it. People have seen him in Limoges in that café where all the Germans go. No true Frenchman would be caught dead there. He's a *collabo*, I tell you. How else do you think he got that fine pair of black leather boots?"

Janine looks around, then tiptoes out silently. Nobody pays attention.

Madame Boulli shrugs her shoulders. "I don't want to know." His father would roll over in his grave if he knew what his oldest

77

son is up to. His father who fought the Germans so bravely in the Great War, back in 1916."

There is a loud cry from one of the girls in the corner of the shed. Everyone rushes over. Genevieve's finger is bleeding from a little piece of shrapnel that was caught in a clump of wool.

Madame Boulli takes her handkerchief and ties it around the girl's bloody finger. "Do be careful girls, you never know what can hurt you," *Madame* reminds them. She looks around and frowns, "Where is Janine?"

TRYSTS

Mademoiselle Gilberte sometimes leaves the child among the tall grasses and tules beyond the berry hedges on the river bank under the low arching trees. She orders the child to take a nap so she can be "all alone" and have time to read her book. The child obediently pretends to go to sleep; *Mademoiselle* might get mean otherwise.

Mademoiselle Gilberte's "book" is her boyfriend, Fritz.

"*Frites*," the child hears her call in a nervous low voice. "*Frites?*" She pronounces his name like *pommes frites*. It makes her giggle. It is the same name as cousin Fritz, who was deported from Paris. But the Fritz who emerged behind the dark thicket was not the cousin. She recognized with a shock the first time she saw him that Fritz was a *Boche*, a German soldier... the enemy!

The child always watched with fascination. Not even grandfather's most vivid fairy tales held her so enthralled. Without knowing why, the child knew it was wrong. She sensed it was dangerous to be so near to a *Boche* those evenings when the slow sun's rays lingered in the sky well past the eighth peal of the church bells.

And the child understood something else; she understood that other dangerous word... *collaborateure*. These secret trysts that usually ended with much scrambling and rushing about to find *Mademoiselle's* missing shoe... it could mean trouble. You were not supposed to be friends with German soldiers. The child was sure of that.

As *Mademoiselle* straightens her skirt, tucks in her chemise, fastens the combs in her hair, the child is assigned to pick off the twigs and leaves that stick to the wool of her yellow sweater from the ground she has laid on. Once they had to come back to look for a silver comb she'd lost the night before. *Mademoiselle* had been furious that the child crawled out of the thicket empty-handed, but stained with berries instead of holding the lost comb. And there is

79

always that peculiar smell to her afterwards... like the smell of the sheep shearers who'd come through the village between Easter and Pentecost.

Mademoiselle Gilberte, the young woman from the provinces, doesn't know the child is Jewish. Only the nun knows. Soeur St. Cybard is more pre-occupied than ever with the endless demands of the villagers who need her help to review documents, locate wounded husbands, obtain travel permits, and write letters to the French Force of the Interior.

"And she must keep the school going with untrained staff," Cook tells anyone who'll listen. The regular staff had been sent on more urgent war effort... "How is Soeur St. Cybard's supposed to cope all by herself?"

At first the child had rather liked *Mademoiselle* Gilberte who wore a tiny gold crucifix around her neck inside her flowered chemise. She had long lashes and very blue eyes. On one of her thin fingers was a ring with a violet purple stone held up by three sharp prongs. Sometimes the child pretended *Mademoiselle* was her secret big sister. *Mademoiselle* ignored her, but she expected no more from someone so pretty and grown-up. *Mademoiselle* only spoke to the older day girls. She didn't like having to be responsible for the child or she wouldn't have left her alone in the small enclosure near the pillared cloister after the day-students went home. Soeur St. Cybard didn't know about this, but she had begun to notice the small girl's thinness and pallor. She commanded *Mademoiselle* to take her for walks in the countryside where the fresh air would be good for *la petite*.

The child has obeyed her parents' rule and has never told her real last name. *Mademoiselle* has no idea. The child has come to understand that the less she tells, the safer. *Mademoiselle* doesn't like to talk with her anyway.

On their walks in the late spring the child combed the meadows for wild flowers imagining *Maman* and *Papa* might arrive that very evening to take her back home. She made nosegays for *Maman* of tiny marguerites, butter cups, coquelicots, bachelor buttons, dandelions, and purple clover. Once, in a friendlier mood, *Mademoiselle* twisted the flowers into a *couronne* for the child's hair.

Sometime after Easter *Mademoiselle* began to walk nearer to the river ordering the girl to nap on the river bank as she disappeared into the greenery. This was how the assignations with Fritz began. The child watched furtively, afraid of being seen. She could hear their voices coming through the thicket on the other side of the shallow stream.

"**Liebchen, komm doch naher...**"

Sounds, words, familiar sounding words! The child's German grandfather said words like those.

"**Schatzjen, setts Dich auf mein Schoss.**"

And in a more urgent tone, "**Komm zu mir... leg dich hinn.**" Then there would be sighs and groans and sometimes sobs as if one of them was hurt; the cries fading into low murmurs, too soft to understand. The child strained her eyes trying to see what they were doing through the thicket. She was afraid but she couldn't keep from looking. She knew she shouldn't be watching. Usually there were too many branches and bushes to see much. Occasionally other soldiers would come by and they would drink from a dark bottle, passing it between them and laughing, though they never seemed to talk much to *Mademoiselle.*

On this very warm evening when she is supposed to be asleep there is a great argument. *Mademoiselle* Gilberte doesn't understand that Fritz had waited for her all the night before by the cemetery. He keeps repeating that she is to come there at midnight on Sunday. Through the dark brambles she sees him shaking her... she is waving her small fist at the tall soldier. Listening to their angry voices she understands exactly what he is trying to say as they shout back and forth, like silly marionettes, neither one of them making sense to the other. *Mademoiselle* gets up, calls him *salot,* runs to where the child lies and they head back home.

Somehow the child wants to help. She waits until they are a good distance from the river. After a few minutes of walking back in their usual silence in the deepening twilight, she begins to explain. "Fritz wants you to meet him behind the wall of the cemetery in the Basse-Ville." *Mademoiselle* acts as if a bomb had dropped between them. She begins to shriek as she grabs the child's arm.

"What do you know about it, you little idiot?"

"He waited for you all night."

By now, they are entering through the back gate to the cloister of the convent. *Mademoiselle's* face is grim as she fastens the ancient latch, then with one swift movement, she turns, and the fist that she had waved at Fritz, comes toward the child. The prongs of her purple ring catch her mouth and she falls backwards onto the gravel path. Everything goes off as if a switch had been flicked... spirals spin from her head... then, a dim light returns. She feels her lip thickening inside as if a smooth fat grape has lodged there.

Sprawled on the ground in the early moonlight, the stone pillar's capitals carved with intertwined monsters seem to come alive. The child cries out as much in fear as in pain. *Mademoiselle* Gilberte, looking scared, pulls her up and shushes her with promises of a dozen wild flower crowns. She promises to spray her with her Houbigant Parfum as soon as they return to their rooms and at last, when the child keeps sobbing, she takes out a crunchy sugar cube from her pocket and pushes it into the child's swelling mouth.

"I have more like this one that you can have..."

"But where do you get them?" she asks, barely able to speak through the sobs and the thickening lip. Sugar cubes were rarer than gold. *Maman* had packed a small sack of them under her nightgown in her valise. She had found them on her first desperate night in the convent. She had tried to make them last as long as possible, but their sweet comfort was irresistible and by the end of that unbearable week, she'd had to go to sleep without them.

"It's none of your business where I get them, I can get all I want." The throbbing of the lip was forgotten.

"Can I have one everyday?" The child drives a hard bargain.

"If you are a good quiet girl."

She nods agreement silently. "You must never," she pronounces the never three times. "You must *never* tell about our walks to the little river. If Soeur St. Cybard asks you, you will tell her we walk by the vineyards and climb to the ruins of the manor house." The child nods more vigorously, glad for the ease of her part of the contract. *Mademoiselle is terribly nervous.*

As if she senses this subtle shift in their relationship *Mademoiselle* commands in her meanest voice:

"You will say you ran into that stone pillar when you were not looking. If you tell I smacked you... the lions, the dogs, and the serpents, especially the snake," she pointed to the Romanesque capitals at the top of the stone pillars. "The ugly beasts will steal you in your sleep and drag you to the *Boches*."

The child looks up again at the writhing monsters eating each other in the sharp illumination of the moonlight and nods vigorously. It won't be hard. She is very good at keeping secrets.

BLOOD

Soeur St. Cybard is always up first. As she dresses, she sometimes watches the child lying quietly asleep on the narrow cot. She smiles to herself. *Curled up like a kitten... la petite. Her color has improved...it's because of Spring.* She thanks God for the return of the beautiful season, *yet the child is so thin... and she's grown more quiet of late... a small ghost.* She crosses herself. Not since the sheep shearing a few weeks ago, can she remember the child smiling or laughing. *The child doesn't complain, yet how homesick she must be. There hasn't been a letter from the parents in a long time, but the mails aren't to be relied on. Perhaps I can telephone Madame LeRoi to hear some news... if the lines have been repaired...* Much as she believes in what the *Maquis* are doing, she wishes they wouldn't tamper with telephone lines whenever she needs them.

The nun is uneasy about the child's parents. Though the child is a French Jew, they are not. Their accent is noticeable and the Vichy government has readily turned over thousands of "foreign" Jews for deportation to appease the occupying Germans. She thinks of the roundup at the *Velodrome d'Hiver*, practically in the shadow of the Eiffel Tower where the first mass arrests of Jews began right after Bastille Day in 1942. Seven thousand people including four thousand children were jammed into that stadium for eight days. *Le grande rafle*, the roundup, was undertaken entirely by her countrymen and executed by hundreds of French police! Then the Jews were taken to a detention camp at Drancy from which they were eventually shipped in cattle cars to Poland to work in labor camps, making room for the next sweep of deportees.

"And what happened to the children, *Mon Dieu*?" She asks God under her breath fingering her beads. "Have the child's parents been caught too?" She can't help worrying.

She remembers the terrible moment last January when the two parents had to say goodbye to her. The father was resolute in his grave voice saying, "As we can no longer protect her, this is what we must do to save her," but the tearful mother had clung to her child unable to let her go... as if she knew this could well be the last embrace. The memory brings a tightness to the nun's chest for she herself had had to hold back tears.

If her parents have been caught in one of the roundups... The nun tries once more to put the thought out of her mind but there hasn't been a letter in nearly a month. As she dresses, she prays *may this war end soon and may the parents be spared.* She fastens her skirt to her waist. It is looser than before. She hadn't noticed. True, she'd been eating less, not to the point that she felt hungry, but to fill one's stomach when others were starving would be indecent.

Soeur St. Cybard did not believe for a moment that the thousands of arrested and deported Jews would return. She herself had heard recent BBC broadcast accounts of the extermination of more than half a million Jews in Poland, yet the Vichy government acted as if the Jewish prisoners were simply sent off to camp to work until the war ended. And most people were too busy worrying about their own lives to give much thought to these tales.

"They don't want to know," she says softly under her breath as she kneels for her morning prayers. There is a new stiffness in her knees that makes the morning prayers an act of prolonged pain.

The stories that the Nazis have experimented with poison gas, torturing, starving, exterminating their victims are considered exaggerations. *"Exaggerations!"*

This morning it's hard to fall into the soothing rhythm of her daybreak ritual. She lets the beads slip through her taut fingers.

"Mon Dieu!" She doesn't want to believe these stories either, but Prosper's report not long ago of the two escapees from Auschwitz told of just such things. *All it does is create a small sensation here or there. Only the underground pays attention.* Not one official paper has yet carried the account.

Who will listen? Communists, the *Maquis,* a few Catholic prelates... a few Protestant leaders, according to Doctor Blanchard.

Hardly anyone wants to think about it, She reminds herself.

She kneels on the little stool facing the crucifix above her bed, presses her hands together and says slowly. "Forgive me, Lord, my faith is not strong enough this morning, forgive me." She crosses herself slowly and stands up to finish dressing.

85

As she slips her headpiece over her hair, she turns her head in the direction of the sleeping child and sees spots of blood on the child's pillow. She rushes over to the little cot, feels the child's forehead. The child rubs her eyes and sees Soeur St. Cybard's anxious face.

Why does she look so upset? Maman... Papa? The child wonders. "What is the matter?"

"*Ma petite*, why is there blood? Is there a tooth readying to come loose?" The child doesn't understand. Soeur St. Cybard says, "Open your mouth!"

The child sits up, clamps her teeth together. *How does she know about the lump?* She works her tongue along the inside of her lip. The grape-sized lump is gone, but she can feel some loose skin that smarts from the tongue's touch.

"Open your mouth, I say." The child remembers well, *Mademoiselle will get mad if...* She opens her mouth, but keeps her teeth closed.

"No tooth missing. Does something feel loose?" The nun asks.

The child runs her finger across her teeth, "*Non*, nothing feels loose." She shakes her head side to side. bowing her head down as she was trained to do.

"Perhaps the blood came from your nose. Look up at me! Come, come, Look up!" The child's head does not move. The nun grasps her chin and raises it firmly. "Look at me! No, I can't see anything. Where can the blood have come from, Josie?"

The child can smell the nun's breath so close up. It is not a good smell. She pulls her head back and to the side ever so slightly.

The child doesn't know what to say. She looks at the pillow with the reddish brown spots. Blood, hers? *From Mademoiselle's ring last night...I won't tell, I promised.* Her throat feels dry. *Is it a sin not to answer the nun's questions? I know the answer, but...* She shivers a little.

The nun looks into the child's ears, looks into her eyes pulling the lids up one at a time as if she expected some answer in them, The child's grey-blue eyes are blank and she seems to be holding her breath, the nun notices.

"*Alors,* this blood is certainly a mystery, *ma petite.*"

**Sylvan and Erna Lévy, née Felsenthal—
Honeymoon, Germany, 1933**

Maman and Josie – Sarreguemines, France. March, 1939.

Josie – shortly after evacuation to Montbron, two years old.

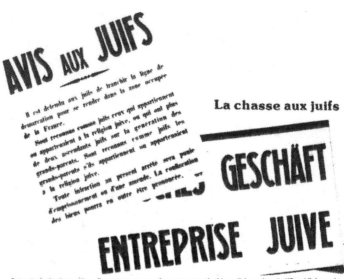

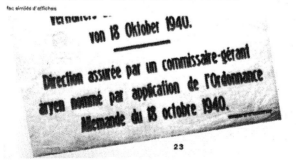

Notice to Jews – "It is forbidden to cross between Occupied & Non-Occupied Zones – Definition of Jewish blood lines "2 grandparents". Below: "Jewish Shop" signs – warning not to patronize. Proof that the Vichy Government collaborated with the Nazis.

**Papa and Maman, Tante Pauline, Uncle Charles, and Josie –
Montbron, summer, 1943**

Papa and Josie by the barn where the Peugeot was kept – Fall 1943.

**Monsieur and Madame LaGarde who allowed the family to
hide at their farm. They also offered to adopt Josie to save
her. Their dog "Mussolini".**

Letter in German to Sylvan's cousin, Max Voythaler, in Massachusetts pleading that Josie be rescued at the end of the war should her parents fail to survive.

Soeur St. Cybard while she served as Directrice of École St. André in Angoulème – circa 1935

Lesterps – the church spire and village date back to circa 990 A.D.

Small street in Lesterps.

An assistant teacher at school with Josie on the front steps of
the school – Spring, 1944. This picture was discovered and
presented to me by the current mayor of Lesterps, Daniel
Soupizet in October, 2000.

The older students at the school. Mademoiselle Guinêt is the
tallest girl standing next to an unidentified nun –
circa 1948-49

Maman's violets that she often wore sprinkled with violet cologne.

Sampler made by Josie with help from the big girls. It was made for Maman, Erna Lévy.

Josie – This photo was taken by an Angoulème photographer to celebrate her return home to Montbron.

Paris, Jardin de Luxembourg – Winter, 1945.

**Maman's passport with Josie's school picture added to it for
the voyage to America.**

**Farewell to France portrait of the Lévy family –
Summer, 1947.**

PAPA'S VISIT

A visitor. When *Mademoiselle* summons her to come to the salon to see him, the child barely says *bonjour*. He puts out his arms, but she doesn't run into them. *It is him...Papa...he's here.*

"*Josielein*, my child, how are you?" His voice trembles.

The sound of his pet name for her makes her smile, just a tiny smile. He takes her in his arms and holds her tight. She stiffens, but she doesn't struggle to get away. *Mademoiselle* leaves the small room without saying anything.

"Let me look at you." His face is too close. She hasn't had any face so close in a long time. She can see the tiny dots of whiskers above his lip. She wishes he would put her down. She wishes he would carry her down the stairs and home.

"You look so pale, *ma petite*, are you eating enough?" He puts her down and sits in the armchair. The child nods and stares and looks down again.

"*Cherie*, look at me," he says in a bewildered voice. She brings her head up slowly, but she can't look in his face. She fixes her eyes on the crucifix behind him on the wall.

"Have you grown a little? Let's see." He stands and puts his flattened hand on her head and brings it to his waist. "Almost up to my belt now. Ah, *Maman* will like it when I tell her that you've grown."

"*Maman*," The word is a big sigh from her mouth.

"Yes," Neither one of them knows what to say next. "*Maman* misses you so much. How happy she would be to see you..." His voice breaks and he turns from her, pulls out his handkerchief, blows his nose several times. Now she looks at *Papa* directly. His bald spot, she'd forgotten about the little circle at the back of his head. The chapel bell rings two o'clock.

"Look here." From his brown coat pocket he takes a little package. Very carefully he unties the thin string on a cardboard box. "*Maman* made these for you." He hands it to her. She nearly drops it. She opens the box and puts her hand inside the brown paper. Moon cookies, the kind *Maman* rolls out and cuts by

106

pressing a heavy glass into the dough, then presses the glass into the circle again to make a perfect half moon. *Maman's moon cookies, here!*

"*Voila*, they didn't crumble. See, they are sprinkled with sugar. Take one." She hesitates. "Go ahead... for you."

Soeur St. Cybard comes in. "Ah, *Monsieur* L'Or, what a surprise. The trains are running today?"

Monsieur L'Or, *Monsieur* L'Or, what a strange name, the child thinks. *Papa is Monsieur L'Or.*

"How is *Madame*?"

"She is helping to care for my father's sick wife. It's very hard, the hospital doesn't take civilians these days."

"To be sure, nothing is as it should be. We put our faith in God. *Alors*, what do you think of our girl?"

The child cringes. Soeur St. Cybard is going to tell the bad things; that she barely eats, that she forgets to look down when adults speak to her. She is a bad girl. *What if she tells Papa about wetting the bed once?*

"She has gotten a little taller, I think," *Papa* says cheerfully.

"It's not possible!" The nun exclaims. "Why, she hardly... *voila*. She is learning well at school, almost like a junior. She has memorized her prayers, the..." Now, the nun pauses a moment uncomfortably. "You understand, of course, *Monsieur*? She is one of us here."

"I... yes, of course." *Papa's* face darkens a bit.

The nun tells the child, "Recite A Child's Prayer. The child begins:

"Angel of God, my guardian dear
To whom God's love entrusts me here
Ever this day be at my side
To light and guard
To rule and guide."

"Very good, Josie." The child does not look at *Papa*. "Now go to the study and bring your reading book here," the nun directs.

When she returns with the green book, the nun turns to *Les Fables De la Fontaine.* "Read this one to your father." It is "The Fox and the Crow." It is only two paragraphs long.

"Once upon a time..." She likes this one best because of the clever fox who tricks the crow to give up the cheese by telling him how beautifully he sings.

"And what is the moral of the fable?" Asks the nun when she finishes reading.

"Every flatterer lives at the expense of his listeners." The child can't read these long words, but she has memorized the moral that they have read aloud so often. She doesn't know what it means. She looks up once to see *Papa*'s face. His eyes shine and his face glows proudly.

The nun continues, "She has been allowed to help with the wool shearing." The child can hardly believe her ears. *Soeur St. Cybard is only telling good things to Papa, how can that be?*

"*Alors*, she is obedient and does what she is told?"

"Quite," the nun replies simply. "*Monsieur*, at what time must you go back?"

Papa looks at his silver watch. "In two hours. The train leaves for Chasseneuil."

"Perhaps you two wish to take a walk, a little promenade to the river or up to the sheep meadows? Wait outside for your *Papa* while I speak with him a few moments," the nun orders.

She does not have to return to afternoon class. She is going to be with *Papa*.

A few minutes later he takes her hand. She leads him toward the sheep meadows. Suddenly he squeezes her hand in his. Three quick squeezes. Without thinking, she squeezes back twice. It is their secret signal whenever they walked together. They laugh. He picks her up in his arms kissing her on both cheeks. This time she doesn't squirm or stiffen, but puts her arms tightly around his neck.

"*Papa*, I want to show you the lambs. When they were born, they were so little. Now they are already getting fat." He lets her down and they walk up the path along high hedges.

"You like lambs?"

"Yes, but I don't like goats. They have sharp horns."

Papa looks hard into her eyes and asks anxiously, "You are very well, isn't that right my child?" She doesn't reply.

They come to a dip in the path. There is a stone cross to the side. The child runs to it, kneels down, crosses herself saying, "In the name of the Father, and of the Son, and of the Holy Spirit."

Her father shakes his head. "Dear Lord, what have we done?" he whispers, looking pained.

"*Papa*, I'm going to pick some buttercups to lay at the foot of the cross for Jesus." She runs into the grassy field happily as he stands and watches her with a puzzled frown. In three months she's already become a little Catholic, he thinks miserably.

They come to a thicket of trees and sit down quietly. He takes out a hand-rolled cigarette, lights it and flicks out the match.

"You didn't let me blow it!" She exclaims.

"I forgot. I'm sor... here, blow this one." After she blows, he says, "Come my little one. Sit here." Shyly she scoots toward him and he puts her on his lap and holds her very close. He smells of tobacco, of new grass, and of sweat. He smells like *Papa*. He rocks her gently.

There are so many things inside... about sitting alone under the nut tree. Jacqueline and Jean Pierre, has *Papa* seen them? She wants to tell him that she is afraid of *Mademoiselle* Gilberte and how beautiful the bells sound inside the chapel. She says nothing. Maybe she will give him the paper cross to take home to *Maman*.

"*Papa*, could we have in our house a... a..."

"What, my child?"

"A little paper, cardboard..." She cannot say the word.

"Come, out with it. What is it?"

"*Rien Papa*. It's nothing." She is quiet.

He takes another puff from his cigarette. She scrambles up from his lap and runs a little distance to where she spots dandelions, cornflowers, lupines, and marguerites. Near a little cluster of trees are some lilies of the valley. She picks so many flowers that she has to gather up her apron to carry them. Then she goes back to *Papa* who is lying on the grass with his hands behind his head.

"Whatever will you do with so many?" he asks.

"I'll make a bouquet." She lays them in piles humming, "Au Claire de la Lune." He whistles along. "I still can't whistle, *Papa*," she tells him in a grave voice.

"You can't?"

"*Non.*"

"Just make your lips round and blow." A perfect clear whistle comes from his mouth. *Doesn't he know that it doesn't work for her?* She purses her lips tightly and blows. No sound. "You're blowing into your mouth instead of out. You have to blow out." Then he yawns and closes his eyes. Sleeping. *Papa* always falls asleep after a promenade. She watches his face. Nothing moves.

She picks the best flowers from the heap on the grass and arranges them into a nosegay. It will be for *Maman*. *Maman* will like a bouquet better than the paper cross. *Papa*'s eyes are still closed. She doesn't like grownups to sleep during the day; it's as if they had left you. *Wake up!* She shakes him.

"Look *Papa*, look at the bouquet I've made for *Maman*."

"What?" His eyes are still closed.

"Flowers for *Maman*."

He sits up slowly stretching. "*Maman?*"

"You can take these home for her. Tell her I picked them."

"In the train? They'll wilt and die."

"They won't die if you hold them up."

"Hold them up?" He looks confused.

What is the matter with Papa? Why doesn't he understand that she wants Maman to have the pretty flowers?

"Just hold them in your hand all the way home. Like this."

She sticks out her arm stiffly. "There, like a candle."

"Oh?"

"A candle... like in the procession when you carry a candle to the altar." Another pained expression comes into his eyes that he blinks away. *What's wrong with him? Why is Papa so slow?*

"I see," he says after a while.

It's not true. He doesn't understand what she means. He doesn't understand about holding the flowers carefully so they'll last for *Maman*. He should understand, but she can tell he doesn't.

110

Why isn't Papa smart enough to... he's supposed to be... She feels a lump in her throat, but she won't cry. She wishes *Papa* would just go back.

Now she feels worse than on those lonely afternoons by the nut tree. *If only I could go on the train and carry home the flowers to Maman myself.* The lump almost chokes her.

Josie Levy Martin

ROCKS

"Your father, what is his name?"

They are walking down a wooded lane toward the old mill when *Mademoiselle* brusquely asks the child. The child blinks but doesn't reply. They walk on a few meters.

"Your father who was here two days ago, *eh?* Come now... what's his name?" *Mademoiselle* repeats.

"*Papa,*"

"*Non,* you little goose, his real name!"

"*Papa,* Sylvain Le—." Her breath slices off the next syllable sharp as a knife, cutting the name in half: 'Le' and silence. The name that always told who she was is no more. It's not even a secret, it's gone.

"Sylvain L'Or," she says quickly to fill the silent place.

"L'Or? Are you sure that is his *nom de famille?*" Without waiting for an answer, *Mademoiselle* adds harshly, "He's not from these parts, is he? Is he French?"

"*Oui Mademoiselle* Gilberte."

"Are you lying?"

"*Non Mademoiselle* Gilberte."

"I don't believe you," her voice rose. "Lying is a sin. Liars are punished. Don't you remember?"

The child says nothing. She wishes they could just go on in their usual silence that *Mademoiselle* prefers on their afternoon promenades. The silence that has become half of her old name is loud now, not calm and soothing like the old silence on their walks. The silence that is now the name is louder than the church bells and the vibrations that take over her body when she helps Soeur St. Cybard ring vespers. From very far down inside she begins to tremble.

Mademoiselle turns to grab the child's chin. "Look into my eyes!" she commands.

A rock that must have rolled onto the dirt lane from the low wall that intersects the fields lays right in the middle of the path. The child, her eyes cast down to avoid more questions, steps

112

carefully around it.   *Mademoiselle* doesn't see the dusty speckled rock. She stumbles.

"Ouuuch!" she shrieks as she tries to keep upright. "*Merde*," she mutters under her breath stopping and taking off her sandal to rub the bruised toe.

The child is aghast. Only once before has she heard anyone say that very bad word. The boy who'd tried to kill the swallow with his slingshot had yelled it after he'd aimed and missed. Without knowing what it meant, the child just knew it was forbidden, but now *Mademoiselle* says it too. The child mouths it without making any sound. Nothing happens. Maybe it's alright to say it outdoors far away from the people that count, far from houses or school. She watches *Mademoiselle* wiggle the toes of her bare foot.

"Hurts, ah... stupid rock!" Slowly, she pulls the big toe apart from the rest. "Not broken, I can move it. *Bien,* I must get down to the stream," she says more to herself than to the child. She slips the foot back into the sandal wincing. "Bend down and fasten the buckle," she orders. "I'm in pain."

The child does as she's told, buckling up the thick strap on the rusty pin. She learned to do buckles from *Madame* L'Abbet, the assistant at the *Ecole Maternelle* in Montbron, but she's still not very good at tying her own shoe laces.

They walk down a little slope in the old quiet silence now. The sound of the stream rushing over the rocks approaching the mill makes a comforting burble. This is a prettier spot than down by the river where they usually walk. Perhaps today they will stop here and be alone and *Mademoiselle* might make a crown from the wild flowers she picks in the nearby meadow. The child recalls the promises of sugar cubes and *couronnes* when *Mademoiselle* hit her mouth.

As soon as they reach the little pond formed by the upper stream, *Mademoiselle* tells the child, "I'm going to soak my foot further down below the mill where the water is colder. You wait here by the clump of reeds. Don't go picking flowers, understand? I want you waiting right here when I come back in a few minutes."

She nods obediently and *Mademoiselle* goes off. The child looks around the lovely spot with little white and grey pebbles lying about and watercress growing at the pond's edge. She collects a pile of stones and throws them in one by one. When the pebble is round and heavy enough it makes a beautiful 'plip-plop' sound like the last few drops of wine bubbling through the narrow bottle's neck into the glass. The sound, when it is just right, sends a delicious shiver, *better than a tickle*, down her back. She can throw the pebbles without hardly moving from the spot *Mademoiselle* told her to wait from.

She gathers more into her careful pile. Sometimes a sluggish snail sticks to the bottom of the rock pulling in its long wormy neck... *Uggh, how can people eat them?* Jacqueline's brother, Jean Pierre, said first the snails are made pure by keeping them in a can without food for twenty-one days. Then they are ready to eat.

She had asked *Papa* if it was true. *Maman* had answered before *Papa* could say anything that snails weren't kosher and that we couldn't eat them no matter how pure. *Kosher, that word, how strange it sounds here by the pond.* "What means kosher?" the child had asked. She remembers *Maman*'s answer spoken in a sad voice.

"It is nothing, nothing."

But *Papa* had followed with, "One day *ma petite*, perhaps one day. You will learn all about kosher."

Another snail, leaving a long slimey trail squirms in the opposite direction from under a large speckled stone when she hears loud words from below the pond, downstream. *Who's shouting? It's a man, Fritz? Not Fritz.* Now the words get angrier, but she can make out only a few of them.

"*Putain*, sleeping with the enemy. You've been seen!" The child carefully creeps down among the tules to get closer to where the voices are coming from. The ground is wet and soggy. She'll get a scolding if her shoes get muddy. She crouches on a fallen log and leans out, holding on to an overhead branch of a low gnarly tree. Fritz is nowhere to be seen. Has he disappeared? *Mademoiselle* Gilberte is standing white-faced. She is not soaking her toe in the water.

A stocky short man in a beret grabs *Mademoiselle*'s shoulder. He shakes her hard, almost knocking her down. *Mademoiselle* tries to pull away, but there is another person, a young...It is the handyman's daughter, Brigitte, who blocks *Mademoiselle*'s way yelling, "Watch out, don't ever let us see you with your *Boches*-Nazi friends again, or you'll find yourself in one of those prison-camps with them."

"*Non*, not a camp... that would be too good for her," the man snaps back. "She'll end up at the bottom of the river one moonless night... salope!" Then he shoves *Mademoiselle* backwards a few steps on the muddy bank. The child can't see *Mademoiselle*'s white face anymore.

"That'll be her lesson, eh Prosper?" The girl mocks.

Bottom of a river, what does he mean? Which river? There are seven big rivers in France that everyone must memorize..They are the Seine, the Loire, the Rhone, the Saone... She can't remember the others. *Maybe he means the Tardoire, the river by Montbron?* Now her breath comes fast. *Dark bottom, mud, snails, snakes...* Both are shouting at *Mademoiselle* who just stands below them, her arms hanging by her sides with both hands rolled into fists.

"Traitor," the girl yells, and spits straight right into *Mademoiselle*'s face.

The child gasps aloud. Then, terrified at the sound she's let out, she scampers frantically through the reeds back up to the little pond. She throws herself down on the ground behind a clump of bulrushes. She presses her hands to her chest to keep the beating inside.

"Please, Jesus, please don't let them find me. Please, don't let them come here... *guarde moi*," she prays to her guardian angel. "Hide me, hide me from the bad people!" She presses her hands over her eyes. *Would Mademoiselle drown if they pushed her into the river? How would I get back? Fritz, maybe Fritz... maybe he will come to save her.* She remembers the long shinny metal thing lying on the grass once when *Mademoiselle* was lying under Fritz.

"Send Fritz," she prays to her guardian angel. Maybe his revolver would scare away all of them and she'd be safe. *Save us* she begs silently, then she sits up on her knees and crosses herself,

115

clasps her hands together and prays: "Help me get back home." The sounds of the little stream pouring into the pond are the same merry gurgle as before. She listens only to it. Her heart's beating slows... it's quiet now. There are no more shouts, not even voices.

A soft swish, footsteps! *Mademoiselle* comes stumbling up through the reeds. She looks... she looks as if all her color has been washed away. Her eyes are more holes than blue. Her light hair is loose from the net that usually holds it in place. The combs are gone. Even her hair going every which way looks scared.

"Hurry up, quick!" she says in a strangled whisper. "Come quick." Her eyes... *Mademoiselle* looks as if she is under a spell. Her eyes are just holes in her pale face. She opens her clenched fists, her thin fingers uncurling and spreading wide at her sides until her whole body shakes. She raises both arms straight out away from her sides as if she is about to fly away... *Mademoiselle, Mademoiselle... she is no longer Mademoiselle...*

"Move along... faster," she hisses.

The child has to run to follow her quick steps along the narrow footpath along the wooded lane, across the wildflower fields, back up the road to the rusty gate of the convent's cloister. *Poor Mademoiselle, she looks so scared.* The child wants to ask her what happened, but she doesn't dare.

They are silent all the way back.

SO MUCH PER HEAD

Doctor Blanchard is in a hurry on this beautiful Sunday morning. He looks anxiously for Soeur St. Cybard to come out of church. The bells peal loudly through the village. Even if he does not go to church, this sound that he has known all his life arouses something. Everything appears so normal in this peaceful village. And though it seems the Germans are losing, the more dangerous it gets.

"*Bonjour, bonjour,*" He touches his hat as people coming down the steps greet him solemnly. "Pardon, Edouard," he taps the stocky handyman on the shoulder. "Has Soeur St. Cybard been to mass this morning? Have I missed her?"

"*Non,* I saw her just a moment ago with the child." Edouard lights his pipe and draws deeply. "Ah, look, there she is just inside the door."

The doctor waits a few moments. There is a fragrance of roses in the air. Roses, jasmine, and mimosa. These gentle signs... Spring has most certainly arrived. The nun with the child at her side comes nearer.

"This is a surprise!" the nun greets him. "Surely, you aren't thinking of coming to mass, Doctor?" She says softly with a faint twinkle in her eye. He ignores the hint of taunt.

"There is news; you should be informed. Perhaps it's true, perhaps it isn't. It doesn't sound good." The doctor moves away from the clusters of people that stand around in their Sunday clothes talking about the fine spring weather. When they are well out of earshot, he says, "I've heard from a friend of my son and also from Prosper."

The child wearing her best light blue challis dress wonders where Mireille Blanchard is on this Sunday morning. Her grandmother did not bring her to mass as usual. She always looks forward to seeing Mireille wearing her deep green velvet dress with the white satin collar. Mireille stands out from the rest of the girls in the small crowd of people in the church pews. And it is not just the beautiful dresses, nor the carefully combed hair with the crisp

117

bows. Maybe it's the way Mireille holds her head up, not noticing anyone else. Usually nobody talks to Mireille after church. She just goes home with her grandmother and probably has to go straight to the study to copy her compositions over.

Gabrielle Sarlat has played with Mireille a few times and reported that she can only play after her work is done perfectly. Mireille is preparing to go to the Lycee in Limoges and she has a tutor who comes every day except Sundays. The child doesn't know what a tutor is, but it sounds serious. She wonders why Mireille doesn't come to school with the other girls of her age.

The doctor is talking very gravely. Perhaps someone is dying and he needs Soeur St. Cybard. The child hopes he won't be talking too long to her. It's hot in her wool dress in the blazing sun.

"Isieu, in the department of Ain," Doctor Blanchard raises one finger sharply in the air. "There was a children's home still being operated by a Jewish Relief Organization. The Gestapo made an early morning raid... they took all forty-one children and the staff of adults. All were deported. Not one has been heard of since."

The nun shakes her head incredulously as she takes in the words.

The child spots Maria a little way behind the fountain. She skips over to the older girl. Soeur St. Cybard has her back to everyone and is facing the doctor intently.

"*Alors*, you are sure?" the nun asks with dismay.

"Very sure. And Prosper says now that the *Maquis* are becoming a real force to be reckoned with, the *Boches* are on a rampage!"

"The Germans know they will lose; they know it's inevitable."

"And they are responding with the rage of the about-to-be-defeated, I'm afraid." The doctor declares.

"God knows what will be," the nun replies. "Worse may yet..."

"The *Maquis* and the *Milice* of course are going at it like never before." The doctor goes on. "It's absolutely dangerous to have anything to do with them now. Imagine, the *Maquis* shot an elderly farmer point blank in broad daylight as he was returning from his field for supposedly having betrayed one of their men to the *Milice*. It's not certain that he did or he didn't. Summary execution, you know."

"One Frenchmen against another." The nun crosses herself. "This is of course only the beginning of the reprisals, retaliations, vengeance! And is this what they will do to the collaborators?"

Suddenly, the doctor shakes his head impatiently. "This is not the biggest problem, let me assure you. The *Boches* aren't done yet. I'm afraid there'll be more of the Nazis' wild abandon once the real retreat from the Allies begins. There are predictions of massacres... a reign of terror." The nun is taken aback by his rising agitation.

He looks around carefully to be sure that nobody is within earshot, especially not the child. "Listen, this is what I've come to tell you. There are Germans who are paying French informants so much per head for every Jew found in the countryside. Those who are hiding Jews don't get off easily either."

"Who told you this, Doctor?"

"A friend of mine, communist from Limoges. He's been involved with the Garel network that has been hiding the children. It's true. There were reports of it in *'L'Humanitee.'*"

"But that was only in the Occupied Zone," she interrupts.

"*Non, non...* **here.** It is happening here! And this time there will be no *Amitiés Chrétiènes* to intervene and come to any children's rescue. Tell me, could your *Mademoiselle* Gilberte possibly know the child is Jewish?"

"Of course not, I'm the only one who..." Now the nun is no longer calm. She explains in an anxious whisper, "The child uses L'or for her last name. I've never heard her use her real one; probably has forgotten it." Beads of sweat form just beneath the fluted brim of her *cornette*. "But why... how? How can you be certain Gilberte is a collaborator?" Her voice drops to barely a whisper as two women pass nearby.

"Unfortunately, I am. You must take my word. Don't ask me anymore."

"*Mon Dieu*," the nun speaks slowly. "I'd hoped they were just idle rumors. Of course, I'm always careful in front of her. She's not from around here, you know. The villagers, everyone is suspicious of strangers."

"I repeat, they are not idle rumors. Now, what will you do?"

Soeur St. Cybard looks stricken.

"I don't think I can dismiss *Mademoiselle* just like that... no, that would call too much attention..."

"Not her, I'm not talking about *Mademoiselle*," he says emphatically. "The child!" He pauses for the nun to comprehend the full import. "What are you going to do about her?" He nods in the child's direction.

"What do you mean... send her away?" The nun is aghast.

"You're in great danger, Soeur St. Cybard, don't you see? Perhaps find her another hiding place."

"*Mon Dieu*, help me..." The nun closes her eyes for an instant. The fragrance of the roses growing along the church wall drifts past on a small breeze. She opens her eyes and looks squarely at the doctor. "I promised her parents. How can I send her away?"

The doctor shrugs impatiently. "Please believe me. For each Jew, man, woman, or child. They are paying so much per head!"

TANT PIS

"*Madame* Blanchard is the prettiest grandmother there ever was," whispers the child as she listens to her reading from the book with the picture of the two boys on the cover. The old lady has soft white hair pulled back loosely into a chignon. Though her face is wrinkled, it has a pinkish glow as if she'd just run up the stairs. Her bright eyes seem to see everything. She is their substitute teacher.

"It is too hot inside, girls. Let us find a shady tree so our brains will not cook," she said shortly after arriving. She led the juniors outside for a reading from the book, *Jean Qui Grogne et Jean Qui Rit.*

"God is good, *Maman*, he will protect us." It is what the cheerful Jean says on the eve before leaving his mother to walk to Paris to seek his fortune. The child tries to imagine such a long walk. They are old-fashioned boys wearing short bloomer pants with wooden shoes and wide brimmed hats. One boy has a big smile with the ribbons on his hat flying up in the air. The other boy sits next to him with his head in his hands and a frown on his face. The ribbons of his hat droop off the brim like two limp noodles.

The child has stared at the cover of the book when she hasn't stared at Mireille's grandmother, dear *Madame* Blanchard. She remembers her own grandmother, *Oma Berthe,* lying against a pillow sick and weak, trying to smile. *Oma* had a bad heart, said *Papa*. She had to go to bed when it was bad. The child asked if a bad heart was like a bad apple. It made all the uncles and aunts laugh when *Oma* told them her grandchild had asked this.

Madame Blanchard wears a purple crocheted vest over a simple grey dress. There is a delicate cameo brooch of a dancing girl with swirling veils pinned to her chest. *Madame* said it is Terpsichore, a muse, not a fairy. The child has never heard of muses and her name is too hard to say. *Madame* also told them she was a teacher at the Lycée, "...in my younger days." Now she has taken charge of the junior girls since *Mademoiselle* Gilberte's mysterious disappearance.

Madame started the day with a cloudy bottle of *eau de toilette* topped with a heart shaped glass stopper. She announced, "I will sprinkle a drop of violets on every girl's handkerchief if it is perfectly clean and ironed." Only three girls had clean enough handkerchiefs in their apron pockets. But the violet scent lingered all morning. Then she began a lesson, not geography, not mathematics, not dictation, not even religion, but a lesson on *la Comtesse de Segur.*

"*La comtesse* is one of our finest French authors and you will see that she loved children. Each of her stories teaches us a lesson, a moral, and God's blessing. She wrote this one for her granddaughter, Marie-Therese de Segur. It is about two boys. One who's always cheerful, and one who always complains. The child listens to her changing voice as she goes from boy to boy. *I wish she could be our teacher forever,* she says to herself.

The mystery of *Mademoiselle* started when she didn't return from her day off last Sunday. Soeur St. Cybard took a long iron key from her big ring to open *Mademoiselle*'s room Monday morning to find out why she didn't answer. The nun came back to the kitchen wide-eyed and confused. She hadn't looked like this since that terrible Thursday afternoon when the child couldn't dictate her letter.

"What, what is it?" Cook asked loudly, holding up the wooden spoon from the bean pot that she was preparing for lunch.

"Not a word, not a note... nothing." The nun held onto the ladder-back chair unsteadily.

"What *did* you find?" The cook asked, letting a few beans roll off the spoon onto the cracked floor.

"All her things gone, not even a hanger in the *guarde-robe.* And the bed, the bed was stripped."

"Those were not her sheets and covers. Why, I just ironed them on Friday after they were brought up by the washerwoman. They belonged here, to the house!" Cook said outraged.

"How could she leave us just like a stranger? Why, she was with us, how long? She came shortly before the child did... more than six months. She came with a solid letter of introduction from the Mother Superior of her school in Poitiers saying she wanted to be a teacher and was of good character."

"I wonder how she got all her things out without our notice. Come to think of it, I hardly ever saw her leave or return. She usually went out at night, didn't she?"

"I'm not sure," Soeur St. Cybard replied slowly. "She was rather private. I didn't ask her many questions."

"You wouldn't have liked her answers," the cook said sharply, stirring the bean pot again. "I heard that she was one of those young women who..."

"Silence!" Under her *cornette* the nun's eyes flashed at the cook with a forbidding stare. "*La petite*, have you forgotten? Not a word of this. I forbid it."

Only the cooking sounds of the bean pot bubbled in the quiet room. Soeur St. Cybard turned to go. "I must speak to Father Gregoire and Doctor Blanchard," she said as she stepped into the hall.

"I've never seen her so..." The cook glanced at the child who was dipping her bread into the bowl of chicory coffee.

"*Tant pis!* Too bad, but never mind."

Cook said *tant pis* all the time like when the beans boiled over or when there weren't enough eggs to make the custard. She said *tant pis* when one of the baby swallows fell out of its nest with a broken wing and it had to be dumped onto the compost at the back of the garden. And when the child knocked a jar off the sink shattering the ceramic pieces, Cook hadn't gotten mad. She just said "*Tant pis!*" *Maman* would have scolded; *Maman* didn't know the word *tant pis*.

By the time the nun returned later in the morning, nearly all the school girls had gathered outside the classroom building. Nobody seemed to mind that the room was still closed. It was a beautiful May morning and Gabrielle had her long jump rope in her knapsack. They were taking their turns one at a time singing.

All in together...
How do you like the weather?
First, second, third, fourth...

The older girls were talking to each other by the stone well about the war and about somebody's father that got captured and taken prisoner. The child took advantage to get more turns at jump rope. This morning she'd jumped up to fifty-one before tripping and having to be a turner. *Mademoiselle* Gilberte never let them play so long.

Finally, Soeur St. Cybard appeared, still frowning and out of breath. She gathered the girls around her and explained there would be no school today, but that they should return tomorrow. A whoop of cheers went up. The child didn't cheer. "Where is *Mademoiselle?*" someone asked.

"She is gone. She will not be back," was all Soeur St. Cybard said.

No Mademoiselle? No school? Now what? The child's eyes burned as if the sun was in them or like when she was about to...

"*Alors,* Girls," Soeur St. Cybard continued. "Tomorrow, *Madame* Solange Blanchard will be your teacher. You may go home now." The girls looked at each other puzzled.

"*Madame* Blanchard?" said Justine to Irene. "Isn't she too old to..."

All in together...
How do you like the weather?

The chant went up once more as the rope circled in its rhythmic slaps against the brick walk. The child did not join in. She ran to the other side of the yard around the corner through an open gate to the enclosure. Alone, she felt her head hot and saw only a blur of blue beige until she clutched the trunk of the little nut tree. She rubbed her eyes expecting them to be wet. There was barely any wetness.

"*Maman...Mademoiselle* Gilberte is gone," She said aloud to the nut tree. "Who will take care of me? She could see *Mademoiselle* in her rose sweater and the flower scarf, and her silver combs... gone. "Did she take the sugar lumps? The sugar lumps she promised me that night when she made the fist and the ring that cut my lip?" And now she remembered how mad *Mademoiselle* would get whenever she accidentally would call her *Maman*.

"I'm not your *Maman*, nor anybody's *maman*. Don't call me that again!"

But sometimes the child would slip and say *maman* without meaning to. And *Mademoiselle* would snap, "Forget *Maman*, you little goose, she's NOT here."

The child nimbly pulled herself up to swing from the lowest branch. She could hear the sing-song of the jump-ropers on the other side of the cloister as the words changed to:

> *Mademoiselle is gone*
> *Mademoiselle is gone*
> *Mademoiselle is gone...*

Suddenly, feeling light as air, she dropped to the ground, and dashed back to the small group of girls still jumping rope.

"*Mademoiselle* took all her things with her," she told Janine who paid no attention. "*Mademoiselle* isn't going to be our teacher anymore!" The child's voice was thin and high to get Janine to listen.

"*Tant pis!*" said Janine as she put up her arms to get ready to jump into the slowly twirling rope.

Now they are sitting in the cool shade of the linden tree listening to *Madame* Blanchard's wonderful voice change from a cheery tone to a groaning whine and back again. The child thinks for a minute about *Mademoiselle*'s low voice calling "*Frittes... Frittes...*" on those twilight evenings. I bet Mademoiselle is with Fritz, she tells herself, remembering how he was always asking her to come with him... or... *those people the other night... maybe she'll come back, maybe not.*

"*Tant pis!*" she whispers under her breath.

125

MAMAN'S LETTER

Saturday afternoon and almost nobody out in the midday heat. The school empties out before lunch. No more classes until Monday. After lunch the child is called into the nun's study. There is a letter from *Maman*.

"It just came this morning, but I see from the postmark that it was sent eight weeks ago. Imagine, two months! Why, that was right after your *Papa* came to visit. The wonder is that the letter came at all."

A letter from *Maman*? The child feels neither good nor bad. The letters don't hold anything of *Maman* in them. Soeur St. Cybard is always so glad when letters come from her parents in Montbron. Maybe that's why her parents send them, to make Soeur St. Cybard glad.

"Listen carefully," the nun begins.

Where is Maman now? Where is Maman this awful hot afternoon? She wonders as the nun unfolds the thin grey lined sheet of paper. *Maman*'s writing is rounder than *Papa*'s. His script is sharp and full of angles. *Maman*'s is full of o's and a's that look like eggs leaning over. One thing she is sure of: *Maman* is not in the letter. The words sound like someone else's; *Maman* didn't talk like her letters. Maybe somebody... another person wrote them like the teacher who lived down the Rue Carnot.

"Chère Josie, Are you being a good girl? I must give you bad news..."

She cannot get a clear picture of *Maman* in her mind, though she remembers the dark blue and white dotted dress and the brown platform shoes... *Maman* sitting at the long kitchen table peeling potatoes or shelling peas. The little scar on her thumb. It's the face she can't see, *Maman*'s face is a blur, like the blur left on her slate after she erases her addition problems. Sometimes she tries hard to bring up *Maman*'s face above the dark polkadot dress, but it just gets fainter.

126

"Sit up straight, Josie, listen well," the nun tells her.

"...I had a fall on my bicycle. I had to have twenty-nine stitches on my face. I broke my collar bone too. Papa was not there..."

Papa is easier to picture. He is taller wearing khaki dungarees and a grey jacket. Sometimes she sees *Papa* lying on his back smoking a cigarette. *Is Papa young or old?* She's not sure. Before, he was just *Papa*, now she wonders why she can't be sure. *I must remember what they look like,* she vows silently, but it doesn't help; their faces disappear into nothing. She tries hard to listen:

"...I still can't move around much. I won't be able visit you because I'm still shakey. I am afraid of the bicycle. I was riding in the countryside. I hit a rock. That's all I remember. A field worker found me fainted on the bike path. The doctor came. I hurt all over. Doctor Dugondier will take the stitches from my elbow and hands. I hope I'll be well again. Be a brave obedient girl, promptly do your lessons and be a good student..."

The letters always have a lot of rules, like *Mademoiselle*'s list to the juniors of what they mustn't do. The child doesn't listen anymore as the nun reads the back of the thin paper.

"Oma Berthe has gotten worse. She sleeps most of the time. I think she has not long to live. Maybe you will not see her again, poor Oma..."

She can see *Oma Berthe* perfectly on her bed leaning back against the puffy white embroidered pillow case.

"Remember your parents. Do everything Soeur St. Cybard says. She is always right."

Love,
Maman

Soeur St. Cybard looks at the child with a small smile. "Well, I'm sure your *Maman*'s stitches have been taken out and now she is perfectly well again."

"Stitches? With a needle and thread in her elbow?"

"It doesn't hurt. The doctor does it." The child cannot understand such a thing. *Stitches like she is learning to do on her sampler? Point de tige, point de cigne, the cross-stitch? A needle piercing through Maman's elbow?* Sometimes during embroidery class Gabrielle Sarlat jabs the needle through the tip of her forefinger and it doesn't bleed, but everybody goes 'Ooooh' and 'Don't' and Gabrielle just laughs. The child cringes and looks pained.

"I'm sure your *Maman* is perfectly well again. That was all a long time ago." The nun says kindly. Soeur St. Cybard doesn't want the child worried. *Why is the child always so still when letters are read to her? And why it is so hard to get the child to dictate a letter back?*

"Do you have anything to say?" she asks. The child casts her eyes even lower and doesn't move.

Where is Maman? Maman is not in that letter that lies on the maroon leather blotter on the big desk. *Maman has forgotten about me. Did she smell the flowers that I sent home for her when Papa came? Maman doesn't even know about the lambs and the swallows... and why doesn't she write them to make me a creme caramel or a tummy-ache soup? Papa said she might send me some sugar cubes. I want them... maybe they've eaten all the sugar cubes. Maybe the chocolate bar up in the cupboard is gone too. I ha... Maman... I hate Papa.*

She is numb.

The nun's voice cuts in. "We're so glad that your *Maman* was not badly hurt, aren't we? The child doesn't even nod her head. "I've asked you a question, *ma petite*. Do you have nothing to say?"

The silence is like in the chapel just before the bells peal. *Je suis Josie L'Or... I am Josie L'Or. They said only a little while... like a day or a week is a little while. It was snowing then. It's hot now, it's summer. Je suis Josie L'Or. I am not their little girl anymore.*

"*Alors*, I am surprised."

Beads of tears trickle out of the child's lowered eyes. She sighs, a silent sob like the brush of a swallow's wing as it alights from a low bough. The nun doesn't see.

"What a strange child you are. You don't think about your *Maman* and *Papa*?"

"*Non*, Soeur St. Cybard," the child answers numbly.

BOCHES

There's a soft knock on the back door. It's Maria, the tall fourteen-year-old with the gentle eyes. She curtsies to Soeur St. Cybard when she enters the study. "Pardon, may I... I'm looking after some of the younger girls for the afternoon. Perhaps *la petite* would like to come on our walk with us? We're picking flowers to take to the cemetery."

"*Oui*, certainly! There is nobody to take her on promenades these days. How very good you are Maria; always thinking of others. There's no girl in the whole school like you," the nun compliments.

Maria blushes, nods, crosses herself. Her thick caramel colored braid wags as she curtsies and backs out the study door awkwardly. Outside four other girls are waiting. The child sees Genevieve and Sabine from the junior class and two smaller girls that she doesn't know. Maria explains, "They are my cousins visiting from the nearby village of Oradour."

Genevieve mimics the village name, "Oradour, dour-dour-dour."

The girls all start to giggle. The child is happy to see the two cousins are smaller than she is. *I won't be la petite this time.*

Maria smiles at them fondly saying, "Solange, Francoise, say *bonjour!*" The little girls grin, but they do not say *bonjour.* One of them is missing a front tooth. They wear matching yellow pinafores with big white ribbon bows in their short hair.

Altogether they walk single file down the cloister steps up the road to the country lane that takes them to the upper meadows. Maria starts to sing a forest song about a cuckoo and an owl:

> *Dans la foret lointaine*
> *On entend the coucou*
> *Du haut de son grand chaine*
> *Il repond au hibou*

Then all voices join in for the chorus of:

Coucou, hibou, coucou, hibou...

The littlest girl shrieks, "Stop, I don't like owls!" and begins to cry. Maria picks her up and tries to soothe her. "It's just a song, the owl is far away in the forest." The other one whines, "Me too... me too... I'm afraid."

"What babies, sissies!" the child says contemptuously to Genevieve and Sabine. "Real Scaredy-Cats! Who ever was afraid of an owl?" She feels very grown-up and important. They wait impatiently as the wailing goes on.

"Maria, we're going to walk up ahead," Sabine calls out.

"Be careful, there are things in the woods... just to the edge where the trees begin." Maria lets them go with a nervous nod.

"I've been in the woods before!" the child brags.

"All by yourself?" both girls ask, wide-eyed.

"*Non*, just with *Mademoiselle* Gilberte... a*t night!*" She says the last two words loudly to make it more important and to make herself brave.

Sabine says, "*Mademoiselle* Gilberte is gone. My brother says she went off with her boyfriend, a *Boche!*"

"I'm going to have a boyfriend when I'm big," Genevieve announces, rolling her eyes with excitement. "My cousin Gaston promised to be my boyfriend when I am twelve."

The child has no idea of what a boyfriend is, but she knows she cannot ask. "Me too, me too," she half chants. *Maybe it's just an older cousin?* "My cousin Robaire is my boyfriend," she declares uncertainly. They all giggle and skip along with their arms outstretched like scarecrows delighted at their escape from the rest. There is a little wind that urges them onward.

Gradually their laughter dies down as they approach the spinney of trees that is much closer now. Beyond the spinney are real woods, tall dark and thickly grown close together. The child looks back in the direction of Maria, but they have walked too far. Maria and the little ones can no longer be seen. The path goes a bit downhill toward a wide shallow ditch that separates the field from the woods. Wildflowers, buttercups, marguerites, and cow parsley grow along the footpath.

In the stillness from behind some rocks, two boys dart out. They are the boys who aimed their slingshots at the swallows a few weeks ago.

"Ah, it's Bernard," says Genevieve in a low murmur, "He's in my brother's class."

"Halt! Halt!" They bark like soldiers.

"Dumb girls!" hoots the tallest one. "They can't come here. This is a danger-zone."

"Yeah, you spies... it's our territory. Nobody's allowed. Get out of here... quick!" He picks up a flat stone and makes a fist. They all look at each other in silence a few long moments.

The medium-sized boy says in a tough voice, "Hey, let's show them the German in the ditch." He gives a boisterous laugh, "That'll teach 'em..."

The tall one looks contemptuous and gives a scornful, "*Zut alors...*"

"Come here, you little goose. You, the skinny one!" The girls stand still as statues in a game of mother-may-I. The child remembers the oldest boy shooting small round pebbles at the baby swallows and how angry *Mademoiselle* was. She wishes *Mademoiselle* were here now.

"Bet you're too scarredy-cat to come," he says in a provocative taunt.

"What for?" Sabine asks with an air of indifference.

"Show you something... something you've never seen before."

"I don't care... I don't want to see something I've never seen before." She turns around as if to walk back.

"What, what is it?" Genevieve asks. Her red-blond curls bob as she nods in her curious fearless way.

"A *Boche*, a dead *Boche*, a Nazi *salaud*... **DEAD!**"

The girls, all three, stiffen. The child gasps, "A dead man? Not dead... I've never seen a dead..." She wishes she could run back. Her knees shake and her stomach rumbles a loud NO.

"What are you, a bunch of scared goose-girls?" He spits on the ground through his teeth like a pirate.

"How... how does he look?" Genevieve blurts out. She is pale as the white iris growing nearby. "I'm not... I'm not scared. Can't hurt us if he's dead." Genevieve is eight, *no wonder she's so brave,* thinks the child.

"You're not going down there!" Sabine speaks without opening her lips. "Are you?" She tries not to cry. "*Mon Dieu,* make them go away..." she prays in a mumble.

Then the three girls, as if they were stitched together by a loose thread, follow the boys.

I won't look, the child promises. *If you make them go away, mon petit ange, I won't look.* She presses her two hands together, but not in a prayer. Everybody would laugh if they knew she was that afraid. *And what if...?* Maybe she has no guardian angel? Refugees have no guardian angels; she had suspected after *Papa's* visit. She sees Genevieve walk with the two boys to the edge of the ditch.

Sabine puts her hands over her eyes saying, "I don't want to see... I don't want to see." The child does the same thing pressing hard against her eyes so that the funny colors appear: a glaze of white, fiery orange, bursts of green... like after you stare at a flame. Then she separates her fingers ever so slightly to see through the cracks. Sabine whimpers softly.

The child follows with her eyes still covered. She crouches a little way off from the three by the ditch. She can see something, but then she presses her fingers over her eyes again.

She hears Genevieve squeal, "Ooooh, sickening... Ooooh, I'm going to vomit." The two boys grab Genevieve's arms so she can't get away.

"Not scared, uh? You said you weren't scared," the big one taunts. "Come on, touch him!" He pulls her hand close to the man lying in the ditch edged in long grasses. A few steps away, Bernard bends over and begins to make funny sounds from his mouth as if something was trying to come out.

His friend looks at him and asks angrily, "What's the matter with you?"

The child's middle fingers spread apart. Now she can see through the greenery. She can see the dead body lying in the mud. *He's so... so young, not like Fritz. He looks like... but it's not, he's younger*

133

than Cousin Robaire! In his muddy worn uniform, he looks like a fallen bronze statue, like the statue of the soldier at the *Place de la Patrie* in Angouleme. He's covered with a thick grayish-green scum, except for his wax-yellow face. Now her stomach feels as if it's going to empty out all over her feet. She stares at his stare. His blue eyes stare, *maybe he's not...* she can't take her eyes off his.

Then her feet take off; she runs back up the rise of the meadow. There are blue corn flowers everywhere. The same color as the dead boy's eyes. She hiccups. A terrible sour taste lurches into the back of her throat, but nothing spills out of her panting mouth. Genevieve comes racing past her at an even faster run with her longer legs. They run and run and run, all the way back to where Sabine was but Sabine is gone. They run one-after-the-other without a sound except for their galloping sandals. When they come around the bend they see Sabine and Maria sitting in the distance with the two little yellow-frocked girls, gathering marguerites and poppies. They slow down to catch their breath. They cannot speak. They can only take in the air. The sweet spring air refills their bodies, crowding out the wretchedness they thought would stay forever.

"Genevieve!" the child says slowly. "Did you, did you?"

"*Oui... Non!* I saw nothing... nothing at all and don't tell!" She adds emphasis to the last words with a shake of curls. Genevieve is calm now. She looks very sure.

They casually approach the little group sitting in the grass. Sabine looks away from them and says nothing. Maria greets them with relief.

"*Voila*, there you are. You didn't go into the woods, did you?" Nobody answers. It is not to be talked about, not to be remembered. Only the sour taste of what rose in the child's throat will be remembered.

"Some very bad things have been going on in the woods in these parts. *Maquis, Millices, Boches...* whatever," and crosses herself immediately.

"I want a crown, make me a crown," the smallest girl begs of Maria and climbs all over her lap like a large pet.

The child looks down at the pile of flowers they've gathered. They are the tricolor flowers: poppies, marguerites, the French flag, but no... there aren't any blue corn flowers. There is not one blue corn flower among them.

REPRISALS

The cherries have left a dark red stain on cook's apron, a huge bruise across her front. The child's fingernails are purple as if she'd dipped them in the ink well sunk into her classroom desk. When she sucks her thumb, she can still taste the sweet flavor of the hundreds of cherries she helped pit for canning. The two sit comfortably at dusk on a stone terrace outside the warm kitchen overlooking the road that passes in front of the convent.

Cicadas sound loudly in the nearby fields. "How do they make that noise?" the child asks. Cook doesn't answer her. "They chirp like birds. I've never seen one, only grasshoppers."

"They're the same as grasshoppers. Don't ask me any more questions. *Mon Dieu*, I'm tired." Cook complains.

"Two days of putting up cherries in jars. Enough! Three dozen... no more!" she tells *Madame* Boulli, who has stopped by to chat on her way back from her kitchen garden. *Madame* Boulli sets down the big watering can that she used to sprinkle the radishes, spinach, and parsley.

"Me too... done in. This hot sun is scorching everything. The baby lettuce hasn't got a chance if I don't water daily... Ah, they look good your preserves," she compliments, as she taps the lid on one of the jars in the first row.

"It's enough to last through winter."

"*IF* we last through the winter," replies *Madame* Boulli. "*Mon Dieu*, it looks grim. They've gone mad, the *Boches*."

"*C'est le nettoyage*... those Nazi pigs. They know they are losing and that the Allies will defeat them after they land. Then it will be all over for them. So they want to clean out the countryside of anybody they say is resisting..."

"*Anybody* in their way. You don't have to be a *Maquis* anymore." *Madame*'s voice rises. "I wish the Allies would land tomorrow."

Cook interrupts; "Wonder if it will be in the South or in the Pas de Calais."

"I heard the mayor say it will be in Normandy," *Madame* says.

"Rumors. That's all we hear... everybody with a new one," Cook folds her arms across her chest as if preparing to sit out whatever was to come.

The child pays no attention to the two women. Instead, she sits nearby, shelling a big basket of peas. She loves this chore and makes a game of guessing how many peas each pod holds. The big fat ones hold six, sometimes seven hard green peas. The slender ones hold only little nodules; she's found out that the smaller the pea, the sweeter. It is the tiny ones she takes for herself. Genevieve brags that the pods in her garden hold ten peas, the child keeps hoping to find a pod with at least eight inside.

"*Alors*," says *Madame*. "We're still lucky they don't come around here. It's worse near Tulles..."

Suddenly she turns her head toward the dark road out front. "Listen... footsteps."

"It's not Soeur St. Cybard, the footfalls are too heavy," Cook mumbles. "A man's, but not my Jules' either; his footsteps are quicker than these." The footsteps sound closer. "Jules comes by to walk me home when I stay late with *la petite*. He worries about me alone. Imagine, after all these years." She gives a little chuckle.

"But he's right. So much going on between the *Millice*, the *Boches*, the *Maquis*. It's dangerous!" *Madame* wags her finger.

A man walking his bicycle in the shadows comes up to the gate. Cook goes down the worn steps to see who it is.

"Ah, *bonsoir* Henri. I thought you were at the meeting with..."

"I was, but I still have my livestock to feed."

"Don't you have help anymore?" Cook asks.

"*Non*, my helper is nowhere around these days. Youngster from Javerdat. He just takes off without a word. Can't count on any of these boys with all the goings on."

"You think he goes underground?" Cook asks in a hushed tone.

"*Non!* Maybe. I don't want to know. I want nothing to do with them. It only means trouble for everybody else." Henri removes his beret and strokes his hair. "I saw him studying a paper on how to put together a Sten gun." Cook gives a little gasp.

"A Sten... like the guns the British have been sending in their parachute drops?" Henri puts his beret back on his head, and shrugs.

"Last week in the barn loft where he sleeps he was listening on a little shortwave to the *Message Personnels*. You know the coded messages that come from across the Channel."

"All the young folk listen to them. All of them think they can break the codes... it's a pastime."

"*Voila*, who knows? Like I said, I don't want to know more." Henri coughs and makes as if to get on his bike.

"*Eh bien*, how long will the town meeting go on?" *Madame* Boulli calls from up the steps.

"A while yet," he answered. "They're still talking about Tulles and what will happen there."

"Tulles, near Brives?"

"*Oui*, south of here." Henri replies tensely. "The *Maquis* took the town and attacked the troops that were garrisoned there. Bloody battle. Over a hundred Nazi troops killed under that daredevil, Chapou. From what they say, hardly lost any of ours."

"*Mon Dieu*," Cook says under her breath again. "How they'll punish the poor townspeople... who can imagine the reprisals?"

"That's the Resistance. Those *Maquis* do what they have to do, then they go back underground and innocent people are left for the reprisals. I have to go. My stock's hungry." He drives off in the moonlight without another word.

"It's all too... too much." Cook says as she climbs the steps back up to the terrace. "Let's see, do I know anybody in Tulles?"

"Don't excite yourself," warns *Madame* Boulli. "Be glad we're not closer to Limoges where they're conducting a real *nettoyage*. They want to clean out all the resisters, but they kill whoever crosses them. All they have to discover is an ambush or a land mine and there's a reprisal; 'search the nearest village and make them pay.' My brother-in-law knew the woman from Bergerac who lived in a little hamlet along the route of one of the Panzer convoys."

"At Les Brégères?"

"*Non,* at Les Bordes, not more than a dozen houses. The commander stopped the convoy on the edge of the hamlet and began to shoot in the air. When he saw the woman in her doorway he demanded, 'Are there *Maquis?—NON—*Whose is this truck standing across the way?—I don't know.' Without asking further, three soldiers jumped out and tore off her clothes."

"*Ah non, Mon Dieu!*" Cook puts her hand over her heart.

"They beat her with their *matraques,* bludgeoning her to a bloody pulp and hung her from the cherry tree beside her house!"

The child shuffles slowly up to Cook with a bowl of freshly shelled peas. "I've done one bowlful. I'm tired. Can I do the others tomorrow?" She is still wearing her earrings from the cherry picking earlier that day. Each ear dangles with triple stems of bright red globes. The color suits her well with her sun-browned face. "I want to go to bed."

"Lie down on the old cane lounge over in the corner. Here, take my sweater to cover yourself." Cook hands her the speckled knit with the tortoise shell buttons. "Ah, *Mademoiselle* will have to remove her earrings," she mocks gently. "You'll drown in cherry juice as you sleep."

The child grins. "When will Soeur St. Cybard be back?" she asks as she heads toward the rickety cane chair.

"I don't know... there are so many meetings now." Cook turns back to *Madame* Boulli. "She feels obliged to attend them. It helps. Some of the older people are excitable, but they listen to her. You know, she is from that order that has as its motto, `Do good and disappear'."

"It's her way and people do like her."

"Indeed," says *Madame* Boulli. "All this talk about abandoning our village at a moment's notice if the Panzers head this way..."

"Shh, please." Cook puts her fingers across her lips.

"*Bonsoir, ma petite.* Go to sleep."

"Just a nap till..." she yawns, then pops the three cherries into her mouth from her left earring. They are warm and sweet; she spits the pits over the low wall of the terrace. The sky is a deep blue, but not dark enough for the stars to lay their cover overhead. She sings the words of *Dans la Foret Lointaine,* as she lies back

139

drowsily. She holds the right earring cherry cluster up above her head. *They're too beautiful to eat. I'll save them for tomorrow.* She hides them in a crack in the wall behind her. Over the edge of the wall she can see the leafy top of the little nut tree in the enclosure below. *Wish I could sleep under my tree and my guardian angel.* She lies down again.

The two women carefully lower their voices.

"After the *Boches* soldiers searched the *Bierlet camion* and found the truck stocked with some food supplies, they approached the houses of Les Bordes. They stopped an old man, a *grandpère*, watering a garden patch with his little grandson. 'Show us the arms you're hiding!' they quizzed the little boy. He said nothing and received a blow from a soldier's truncheon. Then he cried out: 'Maybe there's a gun in the house.' The grandfather grabbed the poor boy, held him to his body and declared, 'There are no arms in the house, none!'

Madame Boulli shook her head as if she still couldn't believe what happened next.

"Two soldiers seized them as others began to beat the old man, but meanwhile a whole truckload of soldiers entered the little cottage and discovered an old English Tommy gun."

Cook gasped, "*Mais non,* every Frenchman who fought in the Great War has some kind of arms... not as weapons, as souvenirs!"

"And so, they beat the old man to death with the boy watching, then set fire to the cottage, and as they got back in their trucks, the commander ordered them to leave, but there was a last shot... and the little boy was no more." *Madame* Boulli's voice cracks as she sobs into her hands.

The child sits up at the sound of the crying. The nearly full moon is still low in the sky, but now there are strips of clouds that cross it. The jasmine that grows along the side of the house envelops the air in its heavy odor. In her drowsiness she cannot remember if she dreamed about a little boy who gets shot, or... *Madame* Boulli cries and cries.

"*Maman,* where are you?" the child shouts across the terrace frightened.

Cook calls out from the low bench at the other end, "*Rien,* nothing. Go back to sleep, *ma petite.* It's nothing at all."

CHAPEL

Soeur St. Cybard comes home after the moon has climbed all the way to the top of the church steeple. "Why does it get smaller?" It was gigantic before. It's a gold earring now, the moon. Why?" The child asks.

Cook does not answer. She only removes her cherry-stained apron and says, "It's late, I must get home."

"Nobody could agree at the meeting because everyone has a different solution. They're all so agitated... I couldn't have taken her along; she's too little to be alone. Thank you for staying," says the nun.

"*De rien,* Sister, it's nothing," Cook replies. "I don't like meetings. People only listen to themselves." She goes down the stairs wearily, her footsteps disappearing slowly into the night.

"Why does the moon get smaller?" The child asks again, then yawns and rubs her eyes, waiting for the answer. Soeur St. Cybard just sits on the plaited chair on the still warm terrace. Her hands are folded in her lap, the rosary hangs down from her waist, its crucifix dangles above the flagstones. She puts her hands over her eyes and the white head piece bobs gently. She stays like this a long time. *What is the matter with her? Why does Soeur St. Cybard sit that way? Maybe it is the time of the grand silence.*

Mademoiselle had explained that nuns have grand silences when they speak only to God. Janine had asked that if there was a fire while they were silent, couldn't they shout, *FIRE! Mademoiselle* had said that they could speak if it was a necessity. 'What if they forgot?' Janine had persisted. Soeur St. Cybard didn't forget. She was ever obedient to God.

The child yawns again and waits for Soeur St. Cybard to take her upstairs to their room so she can go back to sleep on the little cot in the alcove. Her body feels heavy as if it was filled with wet sawdust... like her rag doll felt when she left it out in the rain. Instead, the nun stands up slowly and nods toward the child. A slow clang from the steeple sounds the hour. The child counts aloud: "*Un, deux, trois, qua...*"

"*Non,* not now." the nun interrupts impatiently. "It is the voice of God calling us to pray. Pray for the people of Tulles, that they escape the reprisal that is sure to come. Let us go to chapel."

But it is so late... eleven rings. The child says nothing. Half awake, half asleep she must silently follow Soeur St. Cybard across the cloister under the mysterious moon.

At the door of the chapel, even the two angels with their backs touching and their hands folded in prayer have their eyes closed. Her face is a twist of tiredness. "I'm sleepy," she says outside the chapel door, knowing Soeur St. Cybard is too far away to hear her. She steps over the wooden threshold and into the chapel. The strong smell of spice greets her still wrinkled nose. Father Gregoire must have been here not long ago, sprinkling incense at each station of the cross.

Moonlight streams down through the window behind the small altar right onto Mary in her billowy robes holding Jesus in her arms. Everything else is dark except for the little points of flames coming from the iron candle stand next to the low altar. It is more beautiful to be in the chapel at night than in the daytime.

The Virgin Mary is real... in the moonlight she looks a little shy. "She looks just like Maria when she prays," the child whispers. *If Maria becomes a saint after being a nun, will there be a statue of her in the chapel?*

The holy virgin's lips are parted. *Is she going to talk? Joan of Arc heard voices... they spoke to her... Perhaps tonight... she, the mother of Jesus will talk to me. She might tell me when my Maman...*

The child takes her eyes off the statue and is startled to see Soeur St. Cybard lying face down flat on the floor of the aisle before the large cross that stands just below the altar.

Mon Dieu... what is she doing?

The child has never seen Soeur St. Cybard like this. Her arms are stretched out straight from her body. *She is like a cross.* The silence is terrible as she waits for the nun to get up. She wants to shout at her, *Stand up! Take me to my bed!* She stamps her foot, but Soeur St. Cybard doesn't notice. The needly screech of the crickets is the only sound. "I wanna go home, please... home!" she finally blurts out.

Stiffly, the nun rises up from the stone floor and while still on her knees, prays softly in Latin. Her prayers are always in these mysterious words. *In nominies patrie et filius spiritus sanctus...*

Then changing back to French, she pleads: "Heavenly Father, help me serve thee and thy people. Help us to know when it will be the time to flee. Keep us out of the reach of the enemy. Save us from the terrible fate of our neighbors. Mother of God... *Ave Maria...*"

The child can hardly stand up. She has never been more tired. She leans hard against the back wall of the chapel and slowly slides down against the rough wall until she meets the cool stone floor and sits down. Her head lolls and droops, like Gigi's, her rag doll at home.

A young fellow enters through the side door silently. He lifts one of the burning candles from a candelabra at the back to find his way. In the darkness he nearly stumbles over the child. She stirs in her sleep, her short dress coils around her middle, as she hunches into her usual curl of sleep trying to get comfortable. He backs away from her as one does after almost stepping on a cat.

Soeur St. Cybard looks up and nods at the night bell-ringer.

Slowly she stands and says, *"Bonsoir* Claude, any news?"

"More looting near Saint Junien. They come along in their convoys and help themselves to anything they want... food, livestock... anything. They came to a farmhouse and raided the wine cellar. After helping themselves to several bottles, they locked up the farmer and his family in the barn, then set fire to it." The nun gasps and crosses herself.

The hand holding the candle trembles as the thin boy goes on. He tells it in a hushed voice as if he didn't quite believe the words coming from his lips. "Then, they drove down the road across the farmer's field toward several nearby farms and aimed their automatics at anything in their path... field workers, cows, horses... even dogs; they killed the dogs!" he says, outraged.

"Saint Junien?" Soeur St. Cybard asks. "You're certain?"

"Yes, my cousin and his friend rode their bicycles all the way from St. Maurice over here just two hours ago. They heard about it from folks who were to Etagnac in the afternoon.

"Etagnac?" The nun taps her fingers to her head. *"Oui,* that's on the same road to Saint Junien." Then in a very low voice, "Does Prosper know?"

"I hope so; nobody's sure where he hides... rotten *Boches*... burning to get their hands on him."

"Hush Claude, don't..." Soeur St. Cybard admonishes.

The boy shrugs. "Well, I hope he got word. It travels fast, bad news."

The boy turns away from the nun with his candle casting its light in a bright circle. It flickers from his quick turn and goes out as he walks toward the bell tower.

The nun gives a heavy sigh, and watches him go up anxiously. In some steeples are repositories of weapons... at Siorac, Father Gregoire told her gammon grenades were stored for the *Maquisards*...

She stops herself from conjuring up any more dangerous possibilities and looks around for the child, nudges her up from the hard floor. There is loud barking of dogs from somewhere far off. The nun's coif turns sharply in the direction of the barks. "They never bark at such a late hour," she says to herself.

The child whimpers. She doesn't want to stand up and curls tighter. "Come now, on your feet. *Allez, allez, ma petite.*"

"*Papa,* carry me," the child whines.

"Josie, you must stand on your own two feet." Soeur St. Cybard hardly ever uses her first name. The child scrambles up and clutches the nun's habit. Soeur St. Cybard leads the crying, whimpering girl through the shadowy cloister and up to their bare room. For once, she lets her go to sleep without undressing.

ORADOUR

The big pond is a murky green plateful of pea soup this afternoon. It's so hot the pond might start to boil. The child is trying to stay cool in her quiet spot under a fallen tree nearby. Inside the foliage of the dark green branches she has discovered a small leafy cave that holds one, maybe two people. She might tell Genevieve's brother, Michel, about it and let him join her in this special hiding place. It's a good place to get away from Old Jeanne unnoticed, and sometimes she hears things from her hiding place that the grownups won't talk about if children were near.

Normandie, Oradour, those are the words she keeps hearing over and over. Oradour is why they left the convent a few days ago and why they're hiding in the lower meadows way past where the sheep shearing was done. Everybody says the word 'Oradour' as if it is a terrible secret. Genevieve's *grandmère* starts to cry when they speak of it. Genevieve said it was a village not far away, to the south and that all the people in it are dead.

Normandie is not a village. People are very happy when they talk about Normandie. They say it means the war will soon be over. They say the Germans know for sure they're going to lose now so they are burning up people, and houses, and chickens, and rabbits on their way north.

North is here, the Germans are coming north to fight the Americans and they'll kill everybody on the way to Normandie. That's why they burned up Oradour. *Did the two little girls, Maria's cousins burn?* She had forgotten all about them since they took the walk together. They were such cry-babies.

Lots of people have left Lesterps. "The Germans might come through and burn us all to a crisp," Genevieve announced earlier with a sharp nod of her bright hair.

"Who said?" the child had asked.

"My mother said all the children at Oradour were lined up in the church with their mothers and their grandmothers and their aunts and some of them were babies in carriages and then the Germans set fire to the whole church and all of them burned up."

146

"Solange? Francoise too?"

"Who are they?"

"Maria's cousins, remember? They came on a walk with us on the *Chemins des Pres*," the child explained.

"*Ah Oui*, Solange, Francoise, Maria's cousins, the cry babies... the little girls." Then Genevieve clutched the cross that hung from a chain around her neck and gulped loudly. "*Non, non*, it can't be, not them! They're from Oradour... they... *non, non*, it's not true." Genevieve started crying. She ran to her mother who hugged her. Later, she saw Genevieve all alone praying under a dark oak tree.

Ever since the news of Oradour, people are afraid to stay in Lesterps. Some have gone to other villages, some are hiding on distant farms. Soeur St. Cybard and neighbors near the convent are staying by the pond in the dense thickets that hide them from the main road. The women and children sleep in an abandoned barn on haystrewn floors at night. The men and the boys, when they're around, sleep outside. Everybody is weary, tired, and worried.

Claude, the bell ringer, Henri, and Soeur St. Cybard agreed this was a good spot to hide. "It's far from the *Routes Blanches*, the unpaved roads that the SS Panzer Division uses to bring their convoys to the north," Claude told them.

Claude usually goes off on a heavy clumsy looking bicycle with another boy who wears a long raincoat and a beret no matter what the weather. Sometimes they don't come back until morning, just in time for breakfast. Then the pieces of stale bread have to be cut more thinly to feed them too. Soeur St. Cybard is also gone a lot.

The child is afraid when Soeur St. Cybard is away. *Madame* Boulli explained, "She has to comfort all the poor people who have lost loved ones. She can't just stay here."

"How does she help?" the child asked.

"She helps them offer their sorrows to God," *Madame* says. "Go play and stay out of the way."

The child is miserable, especially because Old Jeanne comes near with that horrible goiter thing and her bad smell. *Why must she always talk to me and call me 'cherie petite.' I hate her.* At night, she tries to sleep as far away from Old Jeanne as possible. Old Jeanne snores and cries words out in her sleep and everybody gets mad. Whenever Old Jeanne heads in her direction, the child runs toward the fallen beech tree and hides in her little cave.

Hortense, Henri and their baby are camped just a little farther off in some undergrowth. Hortense is always nervous that the baby will make too much noise. Last night one of the young men told Hortense that if the little baby fussed, they'd have to tie a cloth around his face. Then Hortense cried.

The child likes to spy on them. Hortense has the biggest breasts she has ever seen. Whenever the baby cries she takes one out of her chemise and stuffs the brown point into the baby's mouth and then he's quiet. Sometimes Henri kisses Hortense and she says, "*Non,* don't..." and then Henri looks mad and goes off.

This morning she watched Hortense nurse the baby while leaning against a tree trunk and talking to Henri, It was about Oradour.

"Baby carriages... bullet holes? It can't be!" Then she hugged her own little baby to her and shuddered.

"The *Sous-Prefet de Rochechouart* and rescue workers found baby carriages with dozens of machine gun bullet holes in the church... It wasn't enough to set them on fire."

"And the babies? What was... left?"

"Nothing, nothing but ashes."

"*Mon Dieu*! At least they won't be orphans."

"Demented dogs! Evil race. They aren't human!" he shouted.

How long will we have to stay out here in the fields by the pond with the fat horseflies? The child wonders. Everybody is all bitten from insects and mosquitoes. They wish it would rain and they could get clean and everything would be fresh again.

Claude has been bringing them the latest news about what has happened in the nearby village and the countryside.

"But why burn Oradour?" Henri demanded. "We expected the reprisal against Tulles as retaliation for the *Maquis'* attack. Why Oradour?" He shook his head and held it in his hands and everything was silent.

148

"I thought I had heard the worst when the Nazis took the mayor hostage and started tossing grenades in the square at Saint Junien to scare the townspeople. All because a few *Maquis* might have been hiding there. But in Oradour there was no resistance... absolutely none. It's too far from everything on those backroads."

"They want to terrify the whole region," said an old woman leaning on a gnarled walking stick. "Me, I'm scared to death." She closed her eyes. Then the baby began to cry loudly and Henri told Hortense to shut him up.

He handed Hortense a small flask from his knapsack and told her, "Give him a little cognac; put him right to sleep." Henri got up, took out a net attached to a rusty metal hoop and headed toward the murky pond. "If I don't catch anything, I'm going back toward town by the river. We have to eat."

Hortense put the flask behind her and began to rock the baby back and forth singing in a quavery voice:

> *Fait do-do, Colin, mon petit frère,*
> *Fait do-do, t'auras du gateaux...*

The child wanted to join in the lullaby the way she did when *Maman* sang it, but then she'd be discovered and the cave wouldn't be her secret anymore. She tries not to think about *Maman*.

In the afternoon Michel shows off the slingshot he's been whittling. "See? It has a thick stump for a handle." Michel is skinny and there are scratches all over his legs. His two front teeth are much bigger than the rest, as if they were the only ones needed.

"And the V is just the right size to tie on the *caoutchouc* rubber for the sling." He whittles on the center branch with a small rusty pocket knife to get all the bark off and make the handle smooth and white.

"Where will you get *caoutchouc* now?" the child asks.

"Claude's going to get me some from an old bike tire. They stuff their tires with bombs and then when they meet a *Boche* they take out the explosives and *Pow*... blow them to pieces!" He jumps off a tree stump straight up and comes down on the ground rolling around a few times. Then he pops upright and asks, "Do you like it?"

"What?"

"My triple somersault. Want to see me do cartwheels?" Michel is always doing wild things and he has treasures in his pockets. He has three orangeade bottle caps. He has a couple of bright marbles. The fattest yellow one he uses only when he has to make the winning shot. He showed her his cartridge shell that he found in a ditch by the railway track.

"But now the trains don't come through anymore because of sabotage."

"What's sabotage?"

"Blowing up bridges and trains and *Pow-Pow-Pow!*" Michel's mouth explodes each time with a spray of spit that makes her jump back. "That's what the *Maquis* do... they sabotage the Nazis, like cutting down all those trees on the highway so their trucks can't get through."

They had to come around lots of fallen trees when they left Lesterps, the child recalls. It was fun to climb over the downed trunks and jump off on the other side. Soeur St. Cybard always went last. She was so slow on account of her long habit. Henri had to hold the baby while Hortense climbed over, then hand the baby to her, then lift his bicycle to the other side, and then he'd climb over and a few meters away they had to do it all again. She tells Michel of the morning before their trek to this place at dawn. It had been like when *Maman* woke her up that other morning long ago, only it was more confusing. Many were scared.

Old Jeanne kept saying, "They're coming to Lesterps. They're coming here next. They're going to burn us up. We're going to be put on fire. Lesterps will burn. We're all going to die!" She said it so often that Henri finally told her if she didn't stop he'd slap her mouth.

Some people wanted to go this way and not by the Rue de Confolens after the word came about the Panzer's advance north to Confolens. Some wanted to bring more things than they could carry.

Cook wouldn't come along. She said she was too old to hide and she didn't believe it was going to happen here. One family got into their Citroen and took off, even though they weren't supposed to have any petro. Some rode on their hay-wagons with their work mules pulling them.

"Everybody got scared because we're on the road to Confolens," said Michel. "But not me. The *Maquis* will stop them. They take the explosives out of the tires of their bikes and stick it in the cow dung or horseshit on the roads."

Michel watches her face to see her reaction. She claps her hand over her mouth. Michel uses that bad word as if nothing would happen. "Then the trucks ride over it and they don't even know what hit them. POW! POW-RAT-TA-TA-TA-TA-TA-BOOM!"

He makes such a noise that she puts her hands over her ears, then quickly takes them down again. Michel might think she's a sissy. Michel is more fun than anybody else. His sister Genevieve just sits around and cries a lot ever since she heard about Solange and Francoise. She's acting serious, like the grownups. But Michel always has something new to tell. He said that maybe he'd teach her to whistle if she didn't act like a scaredy-cat when they go to gather the yellow flowered *pis-en-lis*.

They gather the dandelions and one of the mothers makes a salad out of them, but she only has salt and a little pot of mustard. Still, people are glad to have them to eat with their crusts of bread and their dry chunks of cheese. They eat everything out of their hands. The farmer in the upper meadow has sold them a sack of apples and turnips. The women make turnip soup. The child hates it. Old Jeanne is always hungry and snitches food wherever she can. Michel says Old Jeanne sucks eggs that she steals from the birds' nests.

When Soeur St. Cybard finds out the child and Michel have been going off into the upper fields, she gets angry at Genevieve's mother. "How could you allow these children to wander off alone? There are mines everywhere. Haven't there been terrible mishaps?" Soeur St. Cybard scolds them as well.

"I have enough to do as it is. You will go no further than this side of the pond and you will not wander past the highest oak tree. Do you understand? You could be blown to bits and burned; you'd be nothing but ashes." She grasps the child's trembling chin and pushes her down on the ground. "Both of you, sit for the rest of the day and don't move."

WAITING

Soeur St. Cybard has left with a stranger, a man in a big khaki trench coat from his neck to his shoes, wearing sunglasses and a beret pulled low over his head. The child doesn't know the man. He came on a motorbike and said, "It is urgent." Somebody whispered, "That's Prosper."

By night time Soeur St. Cybard isn't back. The child has refused to eat any supper. No one coaxed her. The soup and the smell of frying fish made her sick. She wanted to go to her little secret place by the fallen tree, but Genevieve's mother said no. Everybody is tired and cranky. Hardly anyone talks. There are only two old men among them. Claude, Henri, and the others are all gone.

She anxiously walks back and forth up the slope to stand by the big oak tree to watch for Soeur St. Cybard. She thinks about the little nut tree in the enclosure that she used to talk to. *Will the Germans hurt my little tree if they come looking to burn more people?* She tries not to cry. *How will the little nut tree hide? Why doesn't Soeur St. Cybard come back?* She looks across the dark fields. The moon is still low on the opposite side of the woods. There is nothing to see. *Where is she? What if she doesn't come back? She was so mad when she left. Maybe she won't come for me.* The child leans against the tree sobbing, "Make her come back, make her come back now. Please, dear Jesus, make her come back." Now she drops to the ground folding her hands in prayer. She hears her sobs that come in spasms. She cannot help them.

After a long time, the sobs slow down. *Maybe Mademoiselle Gilberte will come back... Mademoiselle would get away from Fritz, now that the Germans are going to lose the war and then Mademoiselle won't want to be with Fritz. Maybe she'll want to come back home to the convent and take care of me again.*

"Yoo-hoo, yoo-hoo!" Michel's voice sounds from down behind the barn. "Josie, where are you?" He comes up the wide slope to the tall oak. When he sees her face he will know she is a crybaby.

"Do you want to go catch fireflies?" He asks her as he spots her on the grass. She shakes her head. She doesn't.

"Soeur St. Cybard..." She bites her lip trying not to start crying again. "I'm waiting for..."

"Don't you want to come with me and catch them? They glow. They're like worms."

"I want... I want Soeur St. Cybard to come... to come for..."

Michel doesn't quite know what to do. She's being strange. "Hey, come on, let's go down to the pond. You..." He looks at her exasperated that she is going to cry.

"Michel, Michel, come, where are you?" It is his mother calling now.

"We better get back there," he tells her. "They're mad at us already because of this afternoon. Come on, we gotta go down... they'll probably say it's time to go to bed. *Aww, Merde!*"

That word... that very bad, evil word. Now something bad will happen to them for sure the way Michel says these forbidden things. She never said that terrible dirty word, not even into her pillow.

"*Zut alors,* let's go," he says disgustedly. "No fun, no fun at all."

Michel's mother stands with both hands on her hips, scolding them. "You two... not off again on some escapade, are you?"

Two women sit on a log talking by the shed door with their backs to them. They're talking about Oradour again. It's all anybody talks about.

The one with no front teeth says, "In the baker's oven, the remains of five people... the father, the mother and three children. A whole family put into ovens and burned just as if they were..."

The other woman with a purple wrap around her shoulders interrupts. "The saddest of all are the children, the school children they found in the big church." She wipes her face with the corner of her wrap. "Some of the little ones' bodies were burned, but still clinging to their teachers. *Mon Dieu,* has there ever been anything so terrible? It is as if... God had turned his back on that whole village and loosed the devil on them." Her voice cracks and she starts to pray. The child begins to cry softly.

"Enough of this... the children, Shh!" Genevieve's mother lights a small kerosene lantern and motions to the others to be quiet. "Watch what you say around our own. Be a little more careful, eh?"

Genevieve is already lying down on a dirty cover on the straw by the far wall of the shed. "You can go over by Genevieve," says her mother. "She can probably use some company."

"Soeur St. Cybard, when...?" the child sobs again.

"There now, nothing to cry about. She'll be back before long. She wouldn't like to come home to a crybaby. Dry your tears and go to sleep."

She is in a baby carriage full of ashes. Somebody is pushing it... Old Jeanne. Far ahead, the others are disappearing down the dark lane. She jumps from the carriage and lurches after the ones ahead. Old Jeanne goes after her... *get away... get away from me. Run, run...* her legs are tree trunks; she can't move. She screams, *Papa, Maman, wait for me, please... please... wait for me!* She tries to get the words out loud so they'll hear. Her lips move: *W-A-I-T...* oh wait, no sound... no sound comes out. Old Jeanne is so close behind her now that she can smell her stinky odor... *Maman, Maman...* why won't my legs move? Wait, please wait. She steps on some dark, sticky, slippery mass on the path, it explodes. Her legs turn to ashes. Now she can move, but when she does her legs fly apart into a thousand flakes.

JUNE THIRTEEN

Sun comes streaming down through the chinks in the roof of the old shed on Friday morning. The child stretches on her straw bed; it smells like cut grass. Her head itches. Next to her, Genevieve is still sleeping. Her stomach growls hungrily, she can't remember why she didn't eat last night. Little tiny glints twirl in streams of light that come down through the roof, but when she reaches up her fingers to touch them, there's nothing there. Yet angels come down on such rays of light, she has seen it in pictures. A rooster from a nearby farm crows noisily.

On the far side of the shed, Soeur St. Cybard is kneeling next to a woman, a new stranger sitting on the straw-strewn floor. The woman's face is full of pain. She tells in a voice that sounds as if she is choking: "My only brother, his wife, the two children... nothing left. I saw where their house used to be... burned to the ground, even their animals killed by bullets, only the cat. The murderers... the only one they didn't get was the cat. The cat ran away."

Then her shoulders and her whole body shake so hard she falls against a wood post. She begins to hit her head against it like a hammer. Soeur St. Cybard tries to stop her, another woman rushes over and grabs her by the neck to pull her away from the post. Together they manage to hold onto her to keep her from banging her head. The woman weeps, "Jean, Jean... thirty years old... and the baby... I held him in my arms only a few days before Saturday when I visited."

Henri comes to the doorway of the shed, hands his flask in and says, "Give her some of this to calm her down."

Soeur St. Cybard says quietly, "Dear God, poor woman, back from Oradour. She found nothing; nobody survived, except for this *Madame* Rouffanche." There are tears in Henri's eyes and he walks out. The child crosses herself as Soeur St. Cybard has taught her to do upon rising.

Genevieve is up. She looks around and says, "Let's go outside." It is hot, though the sun's been up only an hour. They walk down to the pond. Michel is there, his feet dangle in the murky water by a clump of low trees. He has a pile of pebbles beside him that he throws one by one as far into the pond as he can. "Guess what? We're going back home."

"To Montbron?" the child asks in a small voice. She looks around fearfully after realizing her mistake. She hasn't told anyone about Montbron. Nobody heard her.

"Who said?" Genevieve asks.

"Claude says it's safe now. The *Maquis* have blocked all the roads, even the *Routes Blanches*. Dirty *Boches* can't get to us. Some people have gone back already."

"But what if they... what if... like in Oradour?" Genevieve asks her brother.

"The *Boches* can't hurt us. The paratroopers are all over the place and the Americans in Normandy with their big guns and big tanks... and they've got enough bombs to blow up all of Germany."

"You don't know everything, Michel." Genevieve tells him.

"Well, it's true and Claude said there's people who go to Oradour everyday to look for bodies. He says they have to wear masks dipped in oil of eucalyptus because it stinks so bad."

"Why does it smell bad?" Genevieve looks at him disbelieving.

"Because it's so hot and it makes dead bodies rot."

The child turns to go back toward the shed. *Madame* Boulli calls to them to come and eat by the big chestnut tree. There is a bucket of fresh milk in a pail and a big loaf of bread on the makeshift table and even some grape leaves with goat cheese. The girls each take two slices of thick bread and a cup of milk and walk over to the fallen tree. They sit on its trunk and eat their breakfast. "I wish there was honey for the bread," says Genevieve as she takes a long drink of milk from her cup. Then she teases, "You have a mustache."

The child wipes her bare arm across her mouth. Cook would get very mad at her for such bad manners if she saw her. She bites off a piece of the delicious bread... the crust is very dark on the underside. That's how she likes it best. Then she gets a painful lump in her throat as she swallows. *Will Cook be there when they go back to the village? What if?* She puts down the rest of the bread and crosses herself again.

"Are you an orphan?" Genevieve asks all of a sudden. The child gasps and shakes her head violently. *Cook will be there when we go back, she always makes potato soup on Fridays.* She can feel her eyes burning, but she isn't going to cry.

Genevieve says again. "Solange and Francoise are dead."

"Are they angels already?"

"Maybe. Only one woman didn't burn up in Oradour." Genevieve swats at a big horsefly that hovers near their food. "*Papa* told *Maman*, she told me. Nobody's left except her, but she broke her leg when she jumped out of the church window above the altar."

"They didn't catch her?" The child asks.

"*Non*, because she crawled to a garden nearby and hid behind the bushes. She hid behind rows of green beans with her broken leg."

Michel comes by and tells his sister to finish up eating so they can go home. He takes out his slingshot and aims it at the horseflies and then makes the sounds of a machine gun. Genevieve yells at him, "Go away Michel, you make too much noise."

"What happened to the woman's leg?" the child wants to know. She wonders, broken where? *Does the leg come off the way a handle comes off a cup? Can you put it back on? Does it hurt much?* She remembers the town crier in Montbron who had a wooden leg. Maybe that was why. Maybe it was because his real leg had broken off.

Genevieve goes on. "Solange and Francoise were in the church."

"Yes... did the woman with the broken leg see them?" The child wants to know.

Genevieve doesn't answer. She finishes her milk and suddenly says, "*Maman* taught me a special prayer to say in difficult times."

Then Genevieve runs up to the big oak tree, drops to her knees, and starts to pray.

Compte les bienfaits de Dieu	Count God's blessings
Mets les tous devant tes yeux	Hold them before you
Tu verras en les comptant	You'll see as you count
Combien le nombre en est grand.	How many they number.

The child doesn't know the prayer. She thinks about counting blessings, but she's not sure what blessings are. She kneels down behind Genevieve and puts her hands together and feels a cooling breeze rustling through the leafy branches.

When she looks up at the sky, she imagines Solange and Francoise with fine white swan-feather wings, flying back and forth in heaven. *Are they still wearing their yellow pinafores? Angels are fatter than the two little girls. They're pudgy like satin pillows. There must be plenty to eat in heaven.* A lot of angels are naked in the pictures she's seen. *Would Solange and Francoise be naked?* She remembers a much older angel in his long robe and golden trumpet, Gabriel. *I wonder if they'll see Gabriel.*

"Are their parents in heaven with them?" She asks Genevieve as they start walking back toward the sheds. They can hear Hortense's baby crying loudly.

"What parents?"

"Solange's and..."

"Oh..." Genevieve isn't too sure, but she nods saying, "Maybe, if their souls are pure; probably, I think so."

"That's good. It's better to be with your parents when you're little," the child tells Genevieve softly.

159

AMI

Ami Entends-tu	*Friend, can you hear*
Le vol noir des corbeaux	*The flight of the ravens*
Sur nos plaines?	*Over our plains?*
Ami, entends-tu	*Friend, can you hear*
Les cris sourds du pays	*The muffled cry of our country*
Qu'on enchaine?	*In chains?*
Ohe! Partisans,	*Ah! Partisans,*
Ouvriers et paysans,	*Workers and peasants,*
C'est l'alarme,	*The alert has sounded*
Ce soir l'ennemi	*This evening the enemy*
Connaitra le prix du sang	*Will learn the price of blood*
Et des larmes.	*And of tears.*

(Song of the Partisans, by Maurice Druon)

Everyone seems to be singing this song all the time, about a friend, a blackbird, blood, and tears. It's a sad song, but when people sing it they sound brave and strong. The child hears it as people walk back to Lesterps. Even on the forbidden radios, it plays again and again. There is one woman that people call the sparrow who sings it, not like a sparrow, but like a soldier who is about to kill.

Snatches of the song drift back to the haywagon on which Soeur St. Cybard, Hortense, and old *Monsieur* Verlain are riding. People at the front of the line returning back to Lesterps sing it as if they weren't afraid anymore. The child wishes she could walk along with the people up ahead, but Soeur St. Cybard said, "*Non.*"

She remembers *Monsieur* LaGarde's wagon in Montbron went a lot faster than this creaky one. It was pulled by Rosette and Ramon, two beautiful black horses. They galloped so fast that trees flew by as you rode. This old mule, named *Escargot*, clops along pulling their wagon more slowly than his name.

The child's head has started to itch ever so often, little bits of straw have stuck to her hair. She crosses herself regularly as they travel. *Cross my heart, cross my arms, cross my fingers.* She makes each finger twist upon the next one as if they were all riding piggy back on each other with the index finger at the bottom and her thumb free. *If I keep my fingers like this all the way home to the village, Cook will be there when we get back. Cook will be there, cook will be there.* It's a chant inside her head the way the *Maquis'* song is a chant. People are talking excitedly to one another.

"*Ah oui*, our *Maquis*, what courage! They're the ones that have saved us." Henri carrying a stick walks alongside the mule talking about how the *Maquis* have driven away the Panzers in another direction by sabotaging all the railways and blocking all the roads. A man with a little black mustache replies, "They've saved us and our whole region now. The Panzers won't dare come near this side of the province cause they can't get their supply trucks through."

Henri hits the mule's side with his whip-like stick. "Oui, that's one of their favorite tricks. Without food, the *Boches* are *foutu!*" says Henri pulling his free hand across his neck in a cutting motion.

The thin man with the mustache tells, "On the day of the Normandy invasion, the *Maquis* started to come out into the open and all the underground cells began to work together. They've liberated Angoulême, Chasseneuill; Limoges will be next. The Charente, Haute Vienne, Dordogne soon will be free."

> "*Ohe! Partisans,*
> *Ouvrier et paysans,*
> *C'est l'alarme...*"

The sounds from the front get louder and the two men clap each other on the shoulders and join in the singing.

Hortense frowns and tells them to be quiet, "The baby's finally sleeping. *Eh la*, the war isn't over yet, don't get cocky."

"Hortense is right," says Soeur St. Cybard. "The Germans may have been driven from here by the *Maquis*, but there are still battles raging. The bombings in Normandy continue," she says in an exhausted voice.

"But Sister," Henri protests sharply. "Now that the Americans have entered, victory is assured, just a matter of time."

161

Vive la France!" says the man with the mustache as he takes a cigarette from behind his ear, licks it and tamps it delicately. "Ah, if only I had a match."

"Where did you get the cigarette, my friend?" Henri asks enviously.

"What do you think? When the *Maquis* ambush the trucks... cigarettes, food tins, all sorts of things." He takes another one, a little flattened from his trouser pocket and offers it to Henri who rolls it fondly. *Papa rolled his cigarettes just like that between his fingers!* The child wonders how can Henri do it exactly the same way.

"It was because of cigarettes that so many perished at Oradour." Henri goes on. "That Saturday was tobacco distribution day. So the smokers came from outlying farms and hamlets to collect their rations. Of course, many brought their families with them to shop and visit."

"And there was to be a medical check-up of all the school children by the mayor's son, Doctor Desourteaux, that afternoon. So all the children had stayed at school instead of going home. The Germans promised them candy and that they'd have their photo taken if they waited calmly." Soeur St. Cybard added in her low voice.

"I just can't understand how they could organize and command so many people to obey, over seven hundred." Henri replies.

"*Mais non,* Henri," says the other man. "They used those *salauds,* the *miliciens,* to translate their orders. The *miliciens* acted like it was a... you know, check the papers, see that everything is in order. Nobody suspected what was to come. Not even the *miliciens.* In the end the *miliciens* were shot in the back when the *Boches* were done with their services."

"Served the damned traitors right!" Henri snaps the stick against the mule's side to urge him to move faster.

Henri's companion continues, "The Mayor suspected as they waited on the *Champ des Foires* that it was something else... insisted that there were no arms hidden anywhere. He offered himself and his four sons as hostages while they searched, if they'd just let the villagers go."

Soeur St. Cybard crosses herself and clutches her rosary beads. All fall silent, but the song from the front floats back.

Ami, entends-tu
Les cris sourds du pays
Qu'on enchaine?

The child watches the baby sleeping. *That's what those angels look like in the pictures, like Hortense's baby. Solange and Francoise couldn't be angels, they were too big.* It made her uneasy. She crosses her heart again with her cramped stiff fingers and the chant in her head grows louder. *Cook will be there, cook will be there.* The hay cart rumbles over rough ground joggling everyone uncomfortably. The mule slows down. In the distance, the vineyards were covered with a delicate green; the bare skeleton-like branches were wearing sleeves. Farmers could be seen hoeing the sandy soil between the rows of vines.

"Not one of those valiant Desourteaux men survived, not one." Soeur St. Cybard whispers and leans against the wide slats of the wooden hay wagon closing her eyes. A tear rolls off her nose.

The child wants to ask Soeur St. Cybard once more if Cook will be there when they get back home. The nun had told her several times that she didn't know and that she should stop asking tiresome questions. The child's fingers are stiff from trying to hold them in the crossed position, but if she lets go, then Cook might not be there when they get back. *I wish Genevieve and Michel were here.*

"Hortense, will Cook be there when we get back?" she asks in a careful whisper, scratching her head with her crossed fingers. Hortense is bending over the baby to brush away the little flies that keep hovering around its face. She doesn't answer her.

DUST

They pass by that bend along the *Route de Confolens* where only a week earlier *Madame* Blanchard and the schoolgirls had left two large bouquets of flowers all wrapped in tri-color ribbon to show the spot where two *Maquisards* had been killed. *Madame* Blanchard had led the little procession and they had kneeled down around the spot to pray for, "our heroic boys." Then they had gently placed the soft flowers where the boys were buried several feet below.

The flowers are just sticks now. They are dead. The wide tricolor ribbon is limp and dusty. The child remembers the dead soldier in the gully down by the river with his shocking blue eyes.

These boys are buried. She gives a little shiver. *Does the dirt get into their eyes if they're buried right into the ground?* She tries to push away the picture of blue eyes muddied by clots of earth, but she can't stop thinking of it. *Does the dirt get into their noses their mouths?* Jaqueline once told her that when you die, after a while you turn into dust and that the wind can blow the dust anywhere.

Dust, *Maman* used to give her a soft rag on Friday afternoons to dust everything just before Sabbath. Then, just as it would turn dark, *Maman*, *Papa*, and she would stand around two little candles stuck up in green glass wine bottles on the table decked with a freshly ironed white cloth. And *Maman* would sing... always the same song in the strange words that *Papa* explained was a blessing. Then *Maman* and *Papa* would each lay their hands on her head and say some more strange words. *Maman*'s hands would linger over the two bright flames as if to protect them and her eyes would fill with tears. Then everybody would say, *"Gut Shabbes"* and kiss each other. And *Papa* would say "I can tell it is *Shabbes* with everything so clean and tidy..."

Will Maman, Papa... will they ever come back? She doesn't know why, but she makes the sign of the cross. Then she scratches a spot just above her neck that has been itching but it doesn't help. *If I didn't bite my nails I could scratch better.*

The hay wagon is rattling along faster as the road dips down toward the village. They are approaching Lesterps. There is the rooftop of *Madame* Boulli's house and the grey slate church steeple. People up ahead are going off in different directions saying *"Adieu, Vive la France!"* as they head home. *Maybe tomorrow we can come back here and bring a new bouquet of flowers for the two Maquisards.* Then she tightly crosses her fingers again... *Cook will be there, Cook will be there.*

Soeur St. Cybard and the child get off the hay wagon after it stops behind the Sarlat's barn. They don't speak as they walk down the narrow street, past the church, toward the priest's house. Father Gregoire sits by the window, eagerly waving at them to stop.

"Thank God, you are all safe and back together again," he says in his thin screechy voice as they come up the grey stone stairs. He stands up to greet them, but falls back in his chair wheezing.

"Where is Cook, Father Gregoire?" the child blurts out the question and then clamps her hand over her mouth surprised that she spoke first.

"Home with her husband. She has been taking very good care of me since Hortense left." He coughs loudly, his bald head turning bright pink.

"Your cough is no better?" Soeur St. Cybard asks sharply. "Are you taking your medicine still?"

He nods, closing his eyes, falls back against the tall arm chair and says in a hoarse whisper, "We will hold a daily mass at five for the victims of Oradour. Each evening the workers try to find and identify the bodies... it is a terrible task. One cannot imagine..." His closed eyes redden as he speaks. "Three of our beloved brothers are still missing."

"Not the two young seminarians?" Soeur St. Cybard gasps.

"*Oui*, and *L'Abbé Jean-Baptiste Chapelle*, my dear old friend." There is a long painful silence. The child scratches her head again. It's as if thin wires were running across her scalp. Father Gregoire goes on. "He had served the parish of Oradour since thirty-three years. First, they thought they had found his body by the burned altar inside the church." The old man takes a deep breath and opens his wet eyes. "Now they are not sure that it was him. They are finding bodies everywhere. Yesterday they found several

165

stuffed in the stone well of the de Lauze farm. The bodies were so brutalized and already decomposed they could not identify them."

Soeur St. Cybard puts her finger to her lips and says softly, "Shh... wait, *la petite*. Go outside child. Wait at the bottom of the steps. I'll come shortly."

The child hops down the stairs in a lively skip, humming a little song to herself. "Cook is back, Cook is back..." She wishes she could wash her hands. Cook will not like seeing her so scruffy and dusty and her hair itchy with straw in it still. She tries to pull apart some of the snarls. Through the open window she can hear Father Gregoire's voice getting louder.

"It is as if God had forsaken Oradour... the *Sous-Prefet de Rochechouart* and the *Doyen de Sain-Junien* were among the first to witness the aftermath..."

"When did they arrive in Oradour?"

"Not until last Monday, the twelfth. The German administration wouldn't let them come near until they'd had a chance to try to cover up some of the worst traces of their brutality. They tried to bury some of the mutilated bodies... didn't do a very good job. Near the cemetery the rescue workers found a man buried in a fresh grave with his hand still sticking out from the earth. When they unearthed him, they found the poor man had his eyes gouged out."

The child takes a stick and traces a hop-scotch grid in the dirt path next to the wall of the parsonage. *What shall I use for a marker?* She looks for a smooth pebble with a nice flat side that won't skip when you aim at the right square. There are no flat pebbles in the border by the parsonage. A thick piece of cardboard makes a good marker. That's what Genevieve always uses. She runs back up the stairs to the house, but stops short. There is a terrible itching of her head. She scratches and scratches, but it doesn't go away.

"They took the host from the tabernacle?" Soeur St. Cybard asks angrily.

"*Oui*, those bandits. Wasn't enough to kill so many innocents. They smashed the altar and the tabernacle after the fire failed to destroy them."

"*Mon Dieu, misericorde!*" Soeur St. Cybard takes a deep breath.

"The Bishop of Limoges has written a letter of protest to General Gleiniger, the German commandant, demanding to know what became of the metal box containing the sacred host." Father Gregoire stands up with his hands clenched. He looks different, younger. He is not wheezing or coughing at all.

"A brave man, our bishop..."

"And then some Germans that came back on Wednesday sneaked back after the rescue workers went home and shot the few remaining live animals, the stray cats, some chickens in their coops... they even stole two bicycles belonging to the rescue workers!" Father Gregoire is furious. "If I was stronger, I know what I would do..."

"Come, don't excite yourself... sit down." Soeur St. Cybard takes the frail man by the shoulders and pushes him back into the armchair. He falls back. His black habit seems to take up more of the chair than he does.

"You know, each evening as the sun goes down, they... the workers hold a mass and bring flowers to the broken tabernacle. The flowers are from the gardens of the dear people who are gone... bones, ashes... dust." Once more the old man closes his eyes. *Has he fallen asleep... or maybe he...* the child stares and wonders uncomfortably.

Soeur St. Cybard turns to go down the stairs. She pays no attention to the child waiting on the threshold. Trembling, the nun crosses herself again and whispers, "Ashes, bones, dust... nothing left but their flowers."

ORPHAN

Cook sees the scruffy girl scratch her head fitfully the minute they enter through the door. She takes her by the shoulder, roughly pulls apart a few strands of hair, and sits her down on a stool, exclaiming as if it was a mortal sin, "*Mon Dieu*, she's full of lice! *Oh la la*, what a mess!"

The child feels awful. *Not a bonjour... nor a smile... she didn't let me hug her when we walked in.* She wants her mother.

Cook only wants to part the child's light sun streaked hair into sections, keeping each one away from the other with wire hairpins, grumbling loudly about how once the lice get into the hair it's hopeless. Soeur St. Cybard looks on uncomfortably.

"They'll be everywhere, all over everything. The cushions, the rugs, the beds, the blankets... it will be like an invasion and we will lose." Soeur St. Cybard says nothing and goes upstairs.

Lice are worse than Boches, worse than Milice, worse than those monsters who burned Oradour, the child thinks shamefully.

When the child was four, *Maman* had her long curls cut off because of the danger of lice. *Papa* had argued, "But couldn't you just wash her head more often?"

"Wash her with what? We don't have enough soap to wash the dishes, nor the clothes."

"Well, make a new batch of it," *Papa* had shouted. "I forbid it. How could you cut her beautiful long, golden curls?" *Papa* loved to twist the slender spirals of hair around his fingers when she sat on his lap for bedtime stories.

"Just make some, eh? And with what, *Monsieur*? We haven't collected enough fat since the last batch. I've been begging the butcher to save me some, but so does everyone... YOU make some," *Maman* told him angrily.

Papa had walked out slamming the door so hard, two tin plates had rolled off the shelf.

"*Papa*... men don't understand the danger of lice... shall I wait until we are all infected and we have to be shaved like them... the ones in the camps?" That same afternoon *Maman* had taken the child to the barber on the *Place de la Mairie* and sitting up high in the barber's chair, the child has watched her tightly spiraled curls drop to the floor, lying there like sad golden sausages. The barber looked sad too and gave her a bonbon afterwards. When *Papa* saw her that evening without her curls, he looked away and acted as if she wasn't there.

Cook declares, "If I don't kill them one by one, we'll have to shave your head and then you'll look like... one of those orphan children in the camps at Drancy. The child has never heard of Drancy, but she's heard of orphans.

"*Voila,* eggs!" Cook yanks on a strand of hair encrusted with nits at the base and holds the scaly scraps under the child's face. "See?" The child barely sees anything... a flake, the tiniest dot of ash. She shakes her head, but Cook starts scraping along her scalp again with her long thumbnail.

"Ouch, oh, it hurts," the child cries out. Cook pays no attention. "Got to get those eggs off if it takes all day. We're not stopping until every last vermin is dead." To make sure, she dips the ends of her fingers into an enamel bowl of water and says, "Drown that vermin... kill them for good!" Then she takes apart the next strand of hair and pulls the thin steel comb through it, though the comb has hardly any space between the teeth, though some of the hair strands are knots and clumps struck with bits of straw.

"Where did you sleep at night, with the pigs? Your hair is full of straw and what else? You smell terrible! I'll have to use the bleach to get the rest of you clean, but not until the delousing is finished. Don't care if it takes until dark. I won't have lice on my girl."

The child's hot tears roll down her cheeks onto the front of her dirty blouse. *I shouldn't have... slept in the straw... should have washed... I forgot...nobody will ever want to come near me again. Not Maman, not Papa, not Jaqueline. Are they ever going to come back?* She wants to get away from Cook. She hates her. *I'll go down to the river and stay in it a long long time and the smell of me will go away...* She wishes she could go sit by herself under the little nut tree. *The tree won't mind my smell.*

"Didn't anybody wash this child nor look at her head? *Voila,* her neck has a week's dirt on it. Clothes are muddied, tattered and her nails... disgusting." Cook mutters as Soeur St. Cybard comes down the hall again from upstairs. She practically accuses the Nun of doing a bad job and neglecting the child.

"Shameful, she looks like... like an orphan!"

That word, orph... orph... The child holds her breath a long time until she can't. *Don't say it...it's like one of those very bad words.* Her shoulders tremble, then her whole body shakes.

Cook looks at her closely now and asks, "Not sick too now are you? Sit still! The way you squirm... wouldn't be surprised if you have fleas too... Soeur St. Cybard sleeping in a barn. Disgraceful! I can't see it! Ridiculous! I told her there was no real danger... told her she could have come to stay in my house, that it was safe enough. But nobody listened to me."

"I don't have fleas," the child sobs. "I want to go, I want my... *Maman...* I'm not an..."

"Only a little more to do and I'll have gotten them all." Cook talks funny with the wire pins stuck in her mouth. "Calm down, child. I'm going to rub you down later with the liquid that disinfects. Soon as the pharmacy opens again we'll get that special ointment and we won't have to shave your head. *Ooh, la la.* Don't cry... we won't have her look like an orphan."

Orphan... the little match girl that was in her picture book at home... the bedraggled beggar-child lying in the snow by a bonfire praying to her grandmother in heaven to take her with her. She stops crying and takes a deep breath. "I'm not an or..."

The word sticks in her throat like a dry cherry pit.

CONFOLENS

It is the end of July, the heat bakes the village stone walls so that even at night they feel warm to the touch. The only cool places are under the little nut tree and down by the river.

"We are leaving Lesterps," the child tells the nut tree as she sits under it, staring up through its dark leaves at the blue spot of sky high above. "We're going to go to Confolens to a real convent where there are lots of little girls and I'm going to live with them in the same room. We'll have our own beds and our own locker to keep our things."

A dry wind rustles the foliage. Two dogs bark at each other in the distance. A shutter from the other side of the yard slams shut as Cook tries to keep the heat out of the kitchen.

"We're going on the train, not in that slow Escargot hay-wagon... a real fast train with our own compartment, just like when *Maman* took me to Limoges." It makes her happy to remember the trip to Limoges. "Soeur St. Cybard is going to be the assistant to the *directrice* and I'll get to live with the juniors."

A bluebottle fly hovers overhead buzzes overhead. *Get away! Uggh, I hate them... uggh, dirty filthy.* Cook always yelled when anyone left the doors open these hot days because flies come on the food. She had hung long sticky streamers from the kitchen rafters and each morning at breakfast, they'd count the dead flies trapped on the waxy streamers. *In Confolens there won't be ugly bluebottle flies, I bet...* "And Maria is going too. She wants to be a nun so she is going to learn how at the big convent in Confolens."

The child had felt lost and frightened when Soeur St. Cybard first explained that they would be leaving Lesterps. An uneasiness came over her. A heaviness in her chest.

How will they find me? I'll be gone far away from here when they come to look for me.

"I've notified *Madame* LeRoi that we are leaving Lesterps and moving to Confolens." Then Soeur St. Cybard began to struggle with words. She couldn't seem to choose the right ones. "If, if your... In case that... If our Lord has deemed in his infinite goodness to save your dear... your..." She closed her eyes briefly the way she always did at grave moments. Then she stood up very erect, explaining quickly, "*Madame* LeRoi will tell your..."

"Is Cook going with us?" The child interrupted.

The nun had already turned away and headed for the door saying, "Better get to the afternoon mass. Father Gregoire can't be kept waiting."

A few days earlier, Cook had talked about Confolens. "*Oh la la.* I've been to Confolens. It's a town, almost a city. It has tall buildings and a streetcar and fine boutiques where rich people buy their clothes. "It's a very nice place, Confolens. Soeur St. Cybard will be much better off there, especially once the war is over."

People were constantly saying, "...once the war is over," or, "...as soon as the fighting stops," or, "...after they liberate Paris."

"How can they tell when the war is over?" she'd asked when Henri had barged into their kitchen.

"The Americans have broken through the German lines at Averanches. It's nearly over, just a matter of days. The *Boches*, they're goners! Dead... finished! Just last week they tried to kill Hitler. Imagine, his own men plotted an assassination! Incredible!"

"Too bad they didn't succeed. Ah me. This calls for a little *aperitif*, Henri." Cook brought a dark green bottle from the salon pouring them each a glass of ruby red wine.

"*A la vôtre!*" They said as they clinked glasses. Cook had taken off her apron and looked gay and happy. "To think, there might really be an end to all this. Nearly five... no, six long years..."

Henri downed his glass, shouted, "*Vive la France!*" and rushed back to his bicycle, riding off in a sort of loopy trail as if the bike had a mind of its own.

Cook took a piece of sugar from the yellow bowl, dipped it in her half empty wine glass and said, "*Voila ma petite.* You must celebrate the good news as well." The child watched the wine soak up to the top of the white sugar, turning it into a bloody colored cube. It was delicious.

"Ah Confolens... I used to go there twice a year before the war to visit my sister Mathilde. She married well, Mathilde... a merchant with a shop of his own... came from Montbron."

"I'm from Mont... *Maman, Papa...*" the child's throat went dry as she tried to ask: "Are *Maman... Pa...* my parents there?"

A fat bluebottle fly buzzed in through the door left open by Henri and landed on the edge of his empty glass. Cook swatted it expertly with her apron. The fly dropped dead on the table, but the glass crashed to the hard floor sending smithereens in every direction.

"*Misericorde,* seven years bad luck!"

"What's seven years bad luck?" *Oncle Charles* always used to say, *The Jews and their bad luck.*

"Out, out! Out you go until I've cleaned up the pieces. Walk on your toes. Mind you don't step on the shards in those flimsy sandals." As the child dawdled, Cook shot back: "No more questions!"

Outside the front door Old Jeanne shuffled by carrying an umbrella over her head. Seeing the child, she beckoned and waved.

"Guess what? The Gypsies are coming!

Why does she always show up when I'm out? The child didn't wave back. She trundled closer to the child by the steps.

"They set up their tents on the *Grande Place. Madame* Vlamink will tell my fortune."

Old Jeanne was awhirl. Her goiter jiggled and quivered as she told of the handsome man *Madame* Vlamink had promised her. "He will have a little brush mustache above his lip... big muscles on his arms. A white satin shirt and he'll play the guitar." She began to sing a familiar melody:

> *Chante, danse la boheme, faria, faria, Oh...*
> *la, la, la, la, la boheme, faria, faria, Oh...*
> *What if all of the money's gone*
> *When you've nothing to spend it on...*
> *La, la, la, la, la, la, la boheme, faria, faria, Oh...*

173

Stupid, Jeanne, doesn't even remember all the words. The child wanted to get away from her, but Old Jeanne went on. "They set up a merry-go-round, our gypsies do, that have painted horses and little carriages, and they have little teeny ponies that you can ride."

"A merry-go-round? A real merry-go-round?" She had never seen one, but Jaqueline had been on one in the park in Angoulème.

Old Jeanne continued, "They play music and they have an organ grinder with a little monkey that has a cup who does tricks if you put a *sou* in it."

"I don't have a *sou*. I don't have any money." The child said unhappily.

"*Voila*, I have a *sou* and some *centimes*." From her dirty apron pocket she handed a copper coin to the child, and though her fingers were black and grubby, the child reached for it and kept it tightly in her fist. "There, now you can ride on the merry-go-round or ride a pony. Here," she reached inside her dress and out came a crumpled franc note and some more coins. "Have another *sou*, have two more *sous*. Know what? The monkey wears a green hat and has a yellow polka-dotted jacket. Cute as a monkey." She laughed at her own joke.

Then suddenly her face grew dark and the lump in her neck hung more heavily as she leaned forward and whispered, "Come closer, *ma petite*."

The child held back, but only an instant. then moved a few steps nearer, tightening her fist, holding the coin. Old Jeanne's smell was strong.

"What, what is it?" she whispered back.

"They steal children... blue-eyed children." Old Jeanne's own eyes nearly popped as she pronounced the last four words. "Blue eyes like... YOU!" Her dirty finger pointed at the child's frightened face.

"Steal children... like me?" the child's voice quavered.

"They steal them and they are never seen again."

"Why, what for? *Non*... you're just talking!" she shouted as Jeanne nodded fiercely up and down. The child backed away. "Honest... for real? It's true?" Her mouth felt dry and she couldn't swallow.

"*Oui,* my little cousine, Anna... she disappeared. Everybody said it was the Gypsies."

Horror swept over the child. In spite of the late afternoon's heat, she felt cold and clammy. She turned and dashed to the kitchen side of the house and hid in the coal chute a few moments until Cook come out to empty the trash.

"What's the matter child? Hunkering in such a dirty place."

"I don't want to go with the Gypsies... I don't..." the child sobbed. "Old Jeanne said..."

"Nonsense, don't you know better than listen to Old Jeanne?" She took the child inside and washed her face scolding, "Crazy Jeanne. Let's see your hands! What's that, two *sous? Eh bien,* wherever did you get those? She give 'em to you?"

The child nodded and sniffled, "Are there Gypsies in Confolens?"

"I should say not." Cook answered most definitely.

"Is there a merry-go-round?"

"A merry-go-round? I'm not, don't remember... oh, why not? Yes, I... there's a merry-go-round in the park."

"Are you coming with us to Confolens?" the child asked, feeling a surge of confidence.

Cook looked out the window at Old Jeanne trudging down the road twirling her yellow umbrella. "Oh that half-wit," she mumbled. "Telling you stories about Gypsies." She cleared her throat and wiped her face. "As if we didn't have enough to worry over *la petite* already."

"Are you coming with us?" The child insisted this time.

"*Oui, oui,* I'm coming too," Cook replied unexpectedly. Then she turned away sharply to cross herself. "*Mon Dieu,* forgive me!" She shook her head slowly blew her nose again, and put her apron back on.

TALK

Michel, Genevieve, and the child are sitting on the church steps this afternoon. Michel's rusty scooter lies on the ground nearby. They are watch the pigeons that come swooping down on the ground to look for food. "Too bad I don't have my slingshot," says Michel.

"They're too skinny to eat... look, the one over there looks like he has a broken wing," his sister tells him.

"I don't care. Kill two or three of them and you can have pigeon soup." He tells her.

"You're crazy. Nobody makes pigeon soup."

"Uh-huh, *potages de pigeon!*" He laughs so loud, the pigeons fly away, circle overhead a few times and land again.

"Go away, Michel! You're an idiot." Genevieve makes a face at him. He makes a worse face in return.

The child watches them with fascination. *I wish I had a brother, I wish I had one.*

Maman had said you can't get babies during the war; that it's too risky. "But *Madame* Marechal got a baby," she had argued with her *Maman*. "They're different, they're not Jew... that's enough," *Maman* had said. "You're too little to understand."

Very close to where she sits, a pigeon with blue-black purple feathers does its quick-stepped walk cooing softly. It is the color of *Madame* Blanchard's earrings, the ones that look like glass grapes dangling on a little gold chain swinging back and forth catching light and sending out rainbows.

"Amethysts," *Madame* Blanchard had corrected when one of the girls had said they were crystal. She wishes *Madame* Blanchard was still teaching. After Oradour, *Madame* had gone to stay with her daughter in Poitiers and had taken Mireille with her. There has been no school since.

Now Michel pulls on Genevieve's braids. She begins to chase; he lets her catch him, but then he runs away again laughing in her reddening face as she tries to grab his shirt. The child wants to be in the chase, but they stop. Genevieve looks furious with her hair going every which way. "I'm going to tell *Maman*," she shouts at him.

"I'm going to tell *Maman*..." he mimics in a silly voice.

"Idiot, brat! You're rotten!" Genevieve bursts into tears.

"Aw, don't cry, aw... *merde*, Genevieve. Stop it! Quit your crying." He's annoyed, but he looks sorry. "I'll give you some of my chewing gum." He offers as he pulls a thick ball of grayish brown stuff from his mouth. Genevieve's tears stop abruptly.

"I want a new piece, you've been chewing on that one for two days."

"I don't have any new pieces."

"What happened to them?"

"In my mouth."

"All of them?"

"*Oui*, but I can get more... when Claude comes back. He'll bring me a bunch, and if you're nice to me, I might give you some." He raises his eyebrows mysteriously.

"Where does Claude get them?" Genevieve wants to know.

"From the American soldiers. The Americans bring them from America. Chewing gum grows on trees over there."

"How do you know?"

"Everybody knows about chewing gum. There's a pink kind too that you can make bubbles with. Claude might get some of that too. He gets gum from the *Maquis*. They get it from the Americans. The Americans are rich, they give away chewing gum, chocolate, anything. Claude is my friend." He says in a way that is as if he's more important because Claude is his friend.

This is the first time the child has seen chewing gum. "You have to chew, but never swallow or you'll choke," Genevieve explains, "And it tastes like peppermint leaves. After a while it stops tasting, but you keep it in your mouth until night-time. Then you stick it someplace until the morning so you can chew it some more."

The child makes a distasteful face, but Michel says, "I chew it like the Americans do..." and he bites down hard a few seconds. Pretty soon there's a wonderful little crack that comes from his mouth.

Genevieve says, "I know how to chew it American too!"

"You do not, you haven't had enough practice... you hardly ever have any gum. Genevieve is about to jump up at him but the child announces:

"We're going to live in Confolens." They stop and look at her.

"I've been to Confolens," says Michel. "It's a real town." He says it respectfully. "It's got a big park with a real lake and little kids set their boats in the water and they have races." Then he adds sheepishly, "It's for little kids; I was helping my cousins."

"Me too," Genevieve added. "And there was a Punch and Judy show in the park, remember? It was so much fun. Judy kept hitting him and he'd disappear and then pop up again and she'd hit him some more."

"Does it have a merry-go-round?" The child asks eagerly.

"Yup, but it's for little kids... doesn't go very fast."

"Does too! You went on it when *Oncle Paul* took us. You rode the unicorn and I rode the dolphin." Michel jumps up and gets on his old scooter with the skate wheels and takes off, calling Genevieve still another name that the child doesn't understand.

"Good riddance!" Genevieve yells. The child is sorry to see him go. Michel is more fun than anyone, but she doesn't say anything to Genevieve about that.

"And after the merry-go-round we went to a *café* where they sell ices, chocolate ices." Genevieve licks her lips and closes her eyes as if she were tasting it right then.

"Chocolate ices?" She remembers *Papa* talking about chocolate ice.

"It's so cold it gives you a headache, but it's so good. You have to eat it fast or it melts into the paper cone... and then it turns into chocolate soup. My cousins had strawberry ices and they had white ones too." Genevieve's eyes shine with the memory of it all. "And my cousins, they have a playhouse... a real playhouse with little chairs and a table and doll dishes with a little teapot. We play in it every time when I go to Confolens."

"Are there dolls in it?"

"*Oui*, you turn them over and they say 'Mama'."

"I have a doll like that," the child says softly. "But she's not here."

"What's her name?"

"Gigi."

Genevieve looks respectful. "Where is Gigi?"

"At home in Mont..." She changes the subject quickly. "Does it cost a lot?"

"What?"

The child is excited about the ices and the merry-go-round. She tells Genevieve, "I have some money..."

"You do? How come?"

"Old Jeanne gave it to me for when the..." she stops to herself. "She gave it to me." The child has the money tied in the bottom of her grey wool sock in her little valise. "I'm going to buy a chocolate ice when I go to Confolens." She can barely wait. She jumps up, twirls on her tip-toes, skips down the steps and runs at the pigeons skimming back and forth looking for food.

BRIGHT MORNING

Boxes of books stand in Soeur St. Cybard's study. The bare shelves look as if they've been undressed. Stacks of letters, papers everywhere threaten to come tumbling down at the least movement of air. There's a brown spot on her large white collar. The child is trying to unknot a loop of string in the long hallway.

"We're going to be leaving for Confolens anytime now," the child heard Cook say yesterday.

Soeur St. Cybard had given Cook a strange look and said, "WE?" Cook closed her eyes and took a big breath.

"Did I hear you right?" Soeur St. Cybard asked in her strictest voice.

Just then Edouard, the handy-man, came in bringing balls of *pale jute* string and two light crates. Cook had rushed to take them from him and moved toward the study.

"Come, please," Cook beckoned to the nun gesturing that she follow her. Cook looked awkward and unhappy. They went into the study and closed the door firmly.

Edouard sat on one of the cane stools, took a long piece of string, tied both ends and twisted it around his fingers making first a long square, then magically, the long square turned into a complicated net. "It's a cat's cradle," he said.

"How do you do it?"

"Easy..."

The child hated it when people said, "easy" about things that were hard. It made her feel dumb... like when she'd asked Genevieve how did Michel make that nice little cracking sound with his gum. All Genevieve said was, "easy."

"Edouard, show me!" The child begged. Edouard paid her no attention. He was busy turning the net into still another grid of clever string work.

"Ah, it's not the way I want it to be... now, how did we used to do that?" With a flick of his wrist, the whole thing fell apart and he was holding nothing more than the loop of string he'd started with.

He took his beret off his head and wiped the sweat with a very crumpled handkerchief. Edouard always smelled of hard work and he never said much.

"Do it again, please, please!" the child begged.

"*Eh bien, voila.*" Once again, his thick fingers made the long square.

"Show me... I want to do it." It seemed like the most important thing in the world to her at that instant.

Edouard looked at her upturned face as if he hadn't really noticed her before. He allowed a rare smile.

"Stand!" He pointed to a place right between his legs.

"Right here, in front of me. No, not like that, turn around." Edouard smelled a little bit of wine and maybe garlic. He pressed her to stand close with her back to him in the triangle of his legs and the string between his two hands. "Put your fingers at the two ends."

The child grasped the string, but as she spread her thumb and forefinger to hold it taut, the whole thing came apart.

"Your fingers are too little. Try again..." She watched him carefully thread up the whole grid once more. *It wasn't magic!* He did it by using his middle fingers and then turning around a certain way... but he did it fast; she couldn't follow.

From the study there were sounds, "Hmm," Edouard said. "A dispute."

The child held out her ten fingers spread wide apart. He carefully wound the string around them. She watched intensely, trying to remember every twist and turn.

The door opened and Soeur St. Cybard said in her less strict voice, "I have my doubts about it, I don't know... and how will I explain... to her?" She sighed deeply.

Cook came out of the study with a very red face as she returned to the stove and tried to coax the embers into a fire, "Almost went out soon as my back's turned, the rascal!" she scolded the stove as always.

The child tried once more to grasp the strings from Edouard's hands. He said he had to go now, but he left her the loop to practice. "But I still don't know how," the child whined.

"She'll show you the way," he pointed at Cook. "She knows these tricks too."

"Not anymore, not with the rheumatism in my hands," she grumbled, poking at the red embers. "Burn you devil!" she ordered the stove.

Now, Sunday, the child sits in the shadowy hall on a stool amidst the boxes practicing with Edouard's loop. Soon Soeur St. Cybard and she will go to mass. At least she knows the first position, but she wishes she hadn't gotten so many knots in the loop. Last night Cook taught her the rectangle. It's the second step that she can't get. Maybe Soeur St. Cybard could show her? The thought makes her giggle, then laugh. *Soeur St. Cybard playing cat's cradle?*

The nun sits nearby with her glasses at the end of her nose reading papers, saying now and then, "Will I need to take this to Confolens with me? Throw this one away child. Put it into the stove bin." It is a quiet morning.

"There's a merry-go-round in Confolens," the child murmurs softly. Soeur St. Cybard ignores her. "And chocolate ice," she says a bit more loudly.

The Sunday morning sun comes streaking through the transom above the door of the hall making that beautiful light-ray ladder on which angels flutter to earth... dust motes drift into the streams forming a slow curtain of silvery sparkles. On the dark floor, a long patch of sunlight shows the cracks and stains of old worn wood.

A knock, not too loud, but long, comes through the door. The child looks up and drops the string loop once more.

"Dumb, stupid!" she blurts out. Before she can pick it up, the knock comes louder.

"*Alors*, child. Go open the door; Cook isn't here right now, you know that." Soeur St. Cybard calls from the study.

She walks down the long hallway on her tiptoes stretching upward to reach the light rays with her fingertips. *Angels never walk on their feet, they skim across space with only their toes touching the floor to make it look normal.* She has to stretch for the doorknob. The iron

182

is rusted and worn like everything in the old building. She turns the bulbous knob stiffly and pulls the heavy door open towards herself. It gives its familiar scraping creak as she looks around it.

There, in the full sunlight stand two strangers.

Maman... Papa.

NUMB

The child gasps as if the wind had been knocked from her small body, stunned! She does not say their names. *Non... both of them, non, not now... they can't be here to take me away just as we're going to Confolens.* She presses her lips firmly together.

Mais NON, non, non, non, non. She is numb with disappointment.

She refuses to look at them so that she just stares and stares at *Maman*'s worn brown shoes. *I don't know them.*

"Josielein, *cherie... bonjour!*" *Papa* is down on one knee and pulls her toward him as *Maman* puts both hands on the child's face. The child stiffens pinching her eyes closed. She turns to stone.

I don't know them. I don't want to go with them... I want to go with Soeur St. Cybard and Cook to the new... with all the other girls and the... For a second she thinks if she would just slam the door back shut she could make her parents disappear.

Soeur St. Cybard rushes down the long hall with her hand extended, "*Bonjour, Monsieur... Bonjour Madame* Lévy. Ah, you made it after all. I didn't know what to expect with the bad roads, the bridges that are out, fallen trees block the crossings." She sees the child pull away from the parents' eager embrace and frowns.

"We came on our bicycles... it took longer than last time." *Papa* explains. "We started yesterday."

"You must be tired, please sit down." She leads them to the salon where they take chairs. Soeur St. Cybard looks at the child severely, noting how she stays back, flattened against the wall in the dark corridor.

"Josie, *viens ici,* come right now. We want to see you." The child hesitates, reluctantly moves a step or two, but refuses to pass through the doorway to enter the little salon. *I won't, I won't, I'm going to run out to my tree... Maman's dress isn't pretty.*

"What do you say? Eh? Your *Maman* and *Papa* are here." The child keeps her lips pressed closed as tightly as if glue had been painted on them and only looks down.

"*Alors*, what kind of manners are these? Say *Bonjour* to your parents." The nun stands expectantly ramrod straight.

After a very long deliberate silence, the child whispers, "*Bonjour*." The nun orders her to look up.

Maman's face is as if it has been slapped. Her mouth opens to say something, but no words come out.

Papa doesn't know what to do. He twists his beret in his two hands and finally speaks, "*Alors*, Soeur St. Cybard, the weather is as nice here as in Montbron... good for the vines... *oui?* They say the grapes are ripening earlier this year because of this hot weather. Be a good harvest for the growers..."

Soeur St. Cybard takes the child's hand and half drags, half pushes the child into the room. "I am ashamed of your conduct," she says just under her breath with her back to the parents.

The child is trying not to cry, keeping her eyes down again, numbly staring at *Maman*'s old brown leather shoes. She feels her cheeks tingle; her eyes burn.

"She's just being shy," the nun tries to explain. "Children are like that sometimes... they talk too much when they shouldn't and become silent when they should... I'm..." She pauses looking at the child's lifeless figure and searches for words.

"She has grown a little, I think... her color is good..." *Maman* speaks, as if from very far away. "*Bien sur*, it's the good air in this region..."

Then they start to talk about the War. It's all that adults ever talk about.

The child stops listening, dazed. Through her burning eyes she fixes on *Maman*'s shoes. She barely breathes. Words jump in and out but they don't mean anything.

...at last, the end of all this seems near...

Thank God.

Have you heard from any of your relatives in the...

They are beginning to tell on the radio broadcasts... terrible things going on.. Soeur St. Cybard shakes her head.

Incredible!

The break-through of the Americans across German lines was a grand triumph... now if only the Allies can land on the Southern Coast of France.

Then maybe the liberation of Paris?

Yes, we have had news from the family that was being held in Gurse and Rives Altes... Maman reports.

Just a matter of time...

My wife's aunt got out over the Pyrenees into Spain, we think she made it to England...

It will end... now we can say that, thank God.

And DeGaulle will be the man for France.

Not a word of my youngest brother...
No news is good news we tell ourselves, the nun tries to reassure.

The Americans and the English... magnificent soldiers...

We have no idea about relatives that got taken away to the East, and... to Dachau... all we do is... hope... God...

For a moment the child listens as she hears *Maman*'s voice crack; she tries to keep it from breaking. Josie looks up at *Maman*'s fine nose and large eyes as they redden. Everyone falls into a respectful silence. Then *Maman* sits up tall again and blows her nose saying, "Come, let us be grateful the war is almost over and all of us... here together again." The tears reappear, but only for an instant. *Maman's French is funny still. She said **le** guerre instead of **la***

186

guerre... Papa still has an accent; it's dumb. She wishes *Maman* and *Papa* would talk right. *Maman* sniffs some more into her handkerchief.

The end, almost the end... everyone says it...

Yes, but there are still pockets here and there... Germans who are trooped in the countryside...and the Maquis, Mon Dieu, some of them will be very unhappy if the war ends too soon...
Yes...

And the collaborators... in our very midst... Mademoiselle...

Mademoiselle Gilberte, I wonder where she is right now? The child is startled as she hears her name mentioned for the first time by Soeur St. Cybard... *Maybe Mademoiselle... she is with her friend Fritz... like Pomme Frittes...* She moves her tongue to the tiny lump in her mouth, from the punch that night that Fritz and *Mademoiselle... Was it long ago? Mademoiselle never came back... she never even said goodbye to me.*
The child begins to count the delicate dust motes that continue to flit up and down the rays of sunlight in the dark hall... *If an angel came down now, right now... Soeur St. Cybard is forgetting that we have to go to Mass. Maybe Maman and Papa will come along and I can show them the baby Jesus and the little basin with the angel and the holy water... and the window above the altar that has that deep blue of iris...*
The adults don't stop talking.
Soeur St. Cybard is telling more about *Mademoiselle... Maman* and *Papa* both look on, disbelieving.
"No of course, I didn't know... I'd never have permitted it... the child may have been in greater danger with me than..."
Maman and *Papa* nod at each other; they are shocked. "She was a Collaborator?"
After a while *Papa* says, "Of course, we were worried when we heard about Oradour. The whole country was, but not a collabo... right here in this..."
Maman is silent.
The church bells ring the hour, nobody moves.

"Amazing, *la petite*. Never told her real name... never gave it away... how I prayed... her guardian angel... I think..." The nun says with a smile in the direction of the child, then she crosses herself closing her eyes.

The child now fixes on the nun's pale face with her eyes closed. *She looks like... white marble... so still and calm...*

Sainte Cybard.

The child presses her hands together as if in prayer.

Opening her eyes, Soeur St. Cybard says in her gravest voice, as from another world, "You entrusted your precious child to me, but in fact, we were to meet the same fate as Oradour... finally, we were in the worst danger possible. It is a miracle, a special kind of miracle that..."

Maman darts up out of her chair, steps across the little salon puts her arms around her child and carries her to the chair and holds her close on her lap.

Maman smells of violets.

EPILOGUE

Memories. What they do to us, what we do with them. A child barely six years old remembers to withhold the name that might have cost her life. And though she tried, the woman that the child became could not forget.

Someone once observed to Primo Levi that his wartime experiences seemed to have been in Technicolor while the rest of his life had been in black and white. It has been like that for me, for many of us. The war, memory in brilliant searing colors becoming strangely more vivid with time; a phenomenon against which all other experiences pale.

I first wrote of my hidden childhood when I was perhaps twelve or thirteen. I wrote it in purple ink in a clumsy scrapbook thick with service club awards, photos, matchbooks and report cards. It was the briefest of accounts, almost an aside. I still wonder why I entered it during this period when all I longed for was to be as American as possible.

I didn't talk about my past outside of home. It was different. I was different, too different... like the bulky hand-knit pullover my mother wanted me to wear when all the girls only wore orlon cardigans.

It was the Fifties. My peers in sunny Los Angeles had no inkling of what had happened, "over there" in Europe. My war experiences were an embarrassment, like my parents' thick European accents. I tried to forget that past along with the French language that had vanished from my tongue. I was no longer that one, "The Child," that quiet sad-eyed child of Lesterps.

Still, that passage in the scrapbook; there it was... something. Perhaps nothing more than an overblown sense of adolescent melodrama because the passage begins with:

"Imagine two parents having to send away their only child, maybe never to see her again."

My mother read it with that mournful look that came over her whenever she remembered the war. I slammed shut the cover of the scrapbook, annoyed at her. By then everything about my parents annoyed me. Their old-world mannerisms, their immigrant coats, their lack of prosperity. We had come in 1947. My father couldn't find work, but my mother found she was pregnant and my brother was born six months after we arrived. We came to Los Angeles because my mother's family had settled here a few years earlier. We didn't fit in the new land, but my mother insisted we loved it when people asked. My father went to citizenship classes and kept hunting for a good job. We were the immigrants, the poor relatives.

By the ninth grade I was obsessed with making myself into Miss All-American, pretended to be in love with Johnnie Ray, Elvis, Little Richard. I went to football games and watched the cheer leaders' every move. I wore a boy's heavy ring on a ball-bearing chain around my neck to look like I was going steady. I earned my own spending money as a baby-sitter. When I was approached by my social studies teacher to become an American Field Service student representative to Europe, I tore up the application. I was *never* going back.

Summers I worked at Newberry's, Mode O'Day, and Sears. I saved every penny. My father was barely earning a living. I had the immigrant's work ethic and I was desperate to go to college after high school. College meant those imposing buildings on the shady USC campus where cashmered girls and golden athletic boys walked hand in hand... a few books under arm. Their casual air was like a spell. I wanted to be one of those beautiful girls. We would drive down Hoover Avenue by the University of Southern California twice a year when we visited *Tante Lina* who lived on Alvarado a few miles away.

Driving past the impressive library, the broad walks, the halls of ivy, even the absurd Tommy Trojan statue, I somehow realized that college was the place where I'd discover what I needed to make it in America. I still can't say how I knew this. I imagined serious study and professors in long robes, students hanging on their every word, and that I belonged among them. Once I asked my parents to tell me the difference between a college and a university.

"Why are you asking?"

"I want to know..."

My mother was at a loss. "Well, it's the university... is like Heidelberg. A college... I don't know, and you don't have to worry about it either."

"But how can I tell which to choose?"

"Listen to her," my mother mumbled in German to my father in the front seat of the old 1935 Buick as if I had been impudent. By my senior year I spoke of college with growing urgency. My parents were silent about it. True, they were proud of my grades, and that I was in the honor society. But it would be a hardship and nobody in the family had gone to higher education. The question hung in the air, heavy as wet laundry on chilly Monday mornings.

Reluctantly my parents allowed it, sacrificing the salary I might have contributed had I started to work. I promised I'd pay my own way. USC was out of the question, but Los Angeles City College only cost six dollars a semester! I could afford it.

An assignment in a freshman class to write a paper reflecting upon early formative experiences. I had to write about the child once more; it was just an assignment. I was determined not to get emotional, just a few pages. Upon handing back the essays, the professor kept mine and read it aloud to the class. There was a long silence and then a trickle of applause.

This was "something" after all.

Then a pert sorority girl sitting nearby whispered, "It's not fair, the rest of us had nothing that good to write about," and she threw me a look of contempt that melted my moment of glory.

There it was, that something, though it couldn't touch me. It was long ago, far way, from another lifetime, even if the child had begun that same afternoon to appear on empty bus benches, stretching out a hand I would not hold. She lingered nearby in a dark doorway sighing; whispering of loss, keening old refrains. The sad-eyed child shadowing my steps as I walked home from the bus along streets lined with fresh tract houses that had no idea... I walked at dusk with a heaviness... a melancholy that would come over me, just a shade, a trace... faint as a fingerprint that couldn't be erased. I turned away.

It didn't matter that I could never be as glad or carefree as my American friends. I still panicked if my parents were even five minutes late coming home. I still had to sneak into churches now and then just to sit before the Virgin Mary. It didn't matter.

It was nothing. The great nothing.

"Something" was those people with the numbers tattooed on their arms. *Tante Lina* who had lost her two children, her husband, and her father in the concentration camps. "Something" was Aunt Ruth who at sixteen had carried her mother on her back across the snow into the woods of a wintry Poland living on dead leaves and trash pickings. My father's cousin's fifteen year old boy had escaped from the very mouth of the crematorium of Auschwitz. Those stories; *they were something...* and in our family, they were as common as the ten-cent phone call.

"What happened to us... compared to Auschwitz," my mother repeated like a dirge, "We... us... it was nothing!"

I had looked up Auschwitz, genocide, concentration camp, crematoria in the New World Encyclopedia when I was twelve. It was all there, all those strange relatives' stories were true. I hated them. How I longed not to be like them and their wounds, to be a real American so that I wouldn't belong to those people and their tales of horror; so that I wouldn't belong to my own. I vowed to be different, to do what none of them could do, get a real education, be somebody.

But the sad-eyed little girl persisted, reappearing unexpectedly under the nut tree on cool afternoons when the clouds were shot with fading light, and always if I had to wait for someone I loved who was late, she would sit by my side trembling.

She came in morning dreams dragging dusty bouquets of wilted flowers that she would scatter over me. I ran, covering my eyes, one arm stretched before me to keep her at bay, but the next night she'd find me again with her dead marguerites, fading cornflowers and red poppies.

I worked harder than ever. No gloomy little girl was admitted into my grown-up scheme. My days were filled with study, work, scrimping, saving to make it through one more year of college, another... and another. There was no time for play and none for sad little girls. So she chased me in dreams, angrily running after me, but always missing the bus that I was on, running out of breath, sobbing. I'd wake up panting. After a few such nightmares, I banished her by sheer will power. That same will power got me through UCLA against great odds, and by the end of four years, I had made it.

Was it a coincidence that I chose a career in which I would be surrounded by children? I doubt it. Something unknown drove me, something undefined, but not accidental. I only knew that if I became a teacher, I would help children, and that it was important; that I would be important.

My vocational choice was a great success. Within three years I became a master-teacher for UCLA, the same university that had trained me. I felt a sense of mission and accomplishment. I remember thinking Soeur St. Cybard would be proud of me.

I loved teaching, but on weekends I was a hippie going to sit-ins, civil rights marches, love-ins. It was the early Sixties. My credo was, "...make love not war." I went on anti-Vietnam demonstrations, wore tie-dyed clothes and handmade sandals. I lived with a hippie artist and his three cats, having rejected a nice Jewish banker businessman, much to the disapproval of my family. My parents were barely speaking to me. I enjoyed their shock and disappointment.

The pale wraith ghost child stayed far, far away in these times.

After the Watts riots in the midst of my idealism, I volunteered to teach at a school in the inner-city. I found myself among neglected, uncared for, battered, suffering children that I couldn't reach or teach. I found it nearly unbearable. Reluctantly, I came to realize that it was almost impossible for me to change the lives of these youngsters. I struggled briefly to hold on and make it work. The damaged children of the ghetto were too many, too hurt, too violent, too sad. Sorrowfully, my idealism went up like the smoke from the fires of the Watts riots. Seven years of teaching and I too was burned out.

In 1968 I took a sabbatical and left for Europe. It was time to return to my German-French beginnings. I was full of eager expectations, as were my aunts and uncles. There were cousins and family friends to visit and renew the ties that had been severed. All had left Montbron in the Charente to return to Alsace-Loraine after the war. Unlike my parents, who were still trying to make it, they had done well. I found them terribly "bourgeois," and they regarded me as an oddity in my hippie clothes. Their stuffiness was proof of hard-won prosperity, just as my psychedelic colored outfits were to show that I was different, no matter how much history we'd shared.

We had not seen each other in more than twenty years. *Tante Rose* wanted me to go to teas with her friends and introduce me to their very proper sons. I begged off. I had been her favorite niece, but now she was disappointed not to find the docile "Josielein" of long ago. We were uncomfortably polite and awkward in each other's company. I couldn't see that there was much between any of us. I stayed with them less than a week.

The rest of Europe was exciting, a memorable stimulating trip, but I'm afraid the reunions were disappointing on both sides. It never occurred to me to look up Soeur St. Cybard.

After my trip to Europe, I returned to graduate school and got a master's degree in child growth and development. The Sixties came to their violent end with assassinations and broken dreams. In 1970 to my parent's great relief, their prodigal daughter married. Not to the hippie-artist, but to a, "respectable" lawyer. I was tired of being different. I welcomed the safety and predictability of marriage. I was in love. I was past thirty and I wanted a family, children. Finally, I thought I would undo the wrongs of my own childhood and indulged in the small conceit that somehow I would be making a worthy contribution to the world by giving my best to children of my own.

During my pregnancy I bought dolls, teddy bears, toys, picture books... I fantasized museum trips, ballets, braces, music lessons, and Erich Fromm's unconditional love. All the wondrous gifts of which I had been deprived would be showered upon this baby.

A few days after our son was born, The Child came back.

First she hovered by the cradle, silent, pointing an accusing finger at him. At night she would push his carriage at breakneck speed toward the river... or she would hide him so that I would search frantically in the woods of troubled sleep. She hid in the nursery behind the butterfly curtains, came and went as she pleased, lurked about like the uninvited fairy, casting evil spells... and I couldn't make her leave. She hung around day and night, hollow-eyed dybbuk, pale wraith, flitting over me as I rocked my baby and tried to sing the Fait Dodo lullaby. I wept and wept. They called it post-partum depression.

She was everywhere like the clouds. She wouldn't be ousted or dispelled. She knocked bottles of formula from my hands, made me lose my way going from one end of the house to the other. I forgot grocery lists, lost car keys, the washing and ironing piled up into heaps. She made the baby fret in his cradle. She was jealous of the silver porringer, of the carved rocking horse, the rosebud blanket. She fiercely resented that he had such adoring parents.

She appeared and vanished... unpredictable as summer breezes. Sometimes I dreamed I'd given birth to unmatched twins; a six-year-old girl who wouldn't speak, and my infant son. I couldn't have been more exhausted; yet at night I tossed and turned fitfully, drifting from woe to desolation.

Finally came lengthy arduous sessions of therapy. The counselor, a large, loving woman, the grand-daughter of a well-known Yiddish poet, gently mothered me in ways I had missed. Sympathy, attention, hugs; long overdue indulgences... all blessings I slowly learned to accept.

She insisted I acknowledge the child I had abandoned so determinedly. She asked me to keep a journal.

I wrote to the sad-eyed child, offering to bargain, make exchanges, small magical gestures. She still wasn't interested. The counselor said the child wasn't ready. Again and again I tried to cast the child out; she stirred up torrents of rage, tantrums... this wild ghost Child.

One day on Sunset Boulevard I found a doll's porcelain tea set with blue forget-me-nots in a second hand store in Echo Park. I bought it for her. We unwrapped it carefully together. She was enchanted!

Lovingly, she washed and arranged each piece in a dozen different ways on a glass shelf in a sunny window. She drank real camomile tea from the cups. It might have been a magic potion, who knows?

I gave her an enameled violet ring, a miniature wind-up merry go-round, and I lent her my box of shiny paints. I bought her an iridescent glass bell, and I made a pretty parasol for her special corner. She played with these for hours and days... a certain quiet fell over us all, gentle reprieve... the hush of slow, slow healing.

We formed a truce. I promised not to forget. I promised not to abandon her ever again.

It took a long, long time.

Much later there was another therapist from South Africa, a German Jew with a deep empathy and understanding of what war did to children. From him I learned that the "great nothing" had indeed been something, something so great I had almost been consumed in the effort to escape it.

I began to write poems, essays, short stories. Stories about strange lonely children, frightened children, wounded children, my pupils, my school children.

There was Katie, the displaced child whose parents' divorce had caused her to live in five foster homes in two years. There was Michael from Harlem who darkened the faces of all the princesses in my Grimm's fairy tale book, "...cause white girls don' be wantin' us black boys." I wrote about the handsome Roger who got caught wearing a dress in the coat-room when he thought everybody was at recess, and about Rebecca, the fat and homely straight-A student who let the cute boys copy her answers in exchange for kisses behind the bungalows. I wrote about Claudia, the autistic six-year-old who had never spoken, but who drew elaborate diagrams of life in outer space, and I had to write about Marco, the nine year old who ran away because the man who had killed his father in Manila was let out of jail.

They were the children who didn't fit... whom I had come to know in the years I was a teacher and later a school psychologist.

Oddly, I didn't set out to write about them. They mysteriously came onto the page, unbidden; a cabal united in some secret design, demanding to be given word-life. A commission I didn't choose to do, but that chose me. In fulfilling this charge of telling their stories, I tried to honor them, give them the place they yearned for, deserved, but had been denied.

As for The Child of Lesterps, after we formed our truce she waited mostly with great patience for her "word life." Not until the external child, my own son was grown and went off to college, was I able to write her singular story. I think I didn't have the courage, the confidence to attend to both at the same time. I suspect that the two of them together would have taken more strength than I possessed.

I never saw Soeur St. Cybard again. I remember nothing of the weeks immediately after my return to Montbron. I am told that I was a stranger; silent, terribly polite, withdrawn. I have no memory of missing the Nun. Did Soeur St. Cybard miss me? My parents did not stay in contact with the Nun after the war. Were they fearful of my attachment to her? Were they afraid that I had become the good Catholic child as they watched me pray to a mysterious guardian angel? What did I pray for? They say I used to stop at every roadside cross and fall to my knees... and that I wandered into churches. The child had been saved, but her soul was elsewhere, roaming, lost.

Soon after coming to America, the state of Israel was founded. I was sent to Hebrew school and learned the remarkable history of the Jewish people; my Catholic ways were forgotten. My Jewish identity was forged, except for secret church visits to see the Virgin Mary. Kneeling before her, I would stare in confused darkness and deep isolation, rushing out almost as soon as I came. Lesterps had become a distant memory.

I wonder if the Nun waited for a letter? A Thursday afternoon letter from the child for whom she had taken such risk? Did she wait for me to return one day all grown up, but full of gratitude and appreciation? I have read accounts and seen films of such reunions between hidden children and their rescuers. I've asked my parents why they did not ever write her, send her a picture of the child she had saved, even long after? They looked puzzled, pained. By then they were already old and felt it was a reproach.

Soeur St. Cybard would have been even older than they, probably not alive anymore. I had waited too long to ask. I would never be able to thank Soeur St. Cybard.

It wasn't that we didn't talk about the war. The subject of our suffering was not taboo as it has been in so many other families. My parents, especially Mother, talked often of our lives during The War, but against the more dramatic events of the Holocaust, against the gasings, the crematoria, the unrecognizable bags of bones that rose from tiers of wooden bunks, barely alive, barely human, I think she felt ashamed to make much of what we endured. For years and years her anecdotes always ended with that brisk angry refrain as when she remembered her beloved Rosenthal china, "Come, let's forget about it... it was nothing."

It was *not* nothing.

I had been a child of war, but I was the one in ten Jewish European children who survived, "the lucky ones," as my mother intoned. I couldn't comprehend the enormity of what it meant. Too often I felt estranged, unworthy, guilty without knowing why or about what. The War and my childhood were inextricably tied together. To disown one meant to dismiss the other. It was impossible. Like the abandoned child who haunted me, the war was ever-present, that bleak, indelible background of a lost childhood. Instead of fading, the images and memories grew more vivid; indeed, Technicolored.

Unknowingly, The War had become that against which all other "terribles" were measured. But at the same time it also established a benchmark of goodness. The War, devastating as it had been, had also been for me, through Soeur St. Cybard, an experience of a rare kind of moral conduct against which I would forever compare all other virtue.

And so, for me <u>both</u> good and evil were strangely imbedded in the war. A confusing duality that caused me deep discomfort and profound humility, for as I grow older this duality, this paradox seems to be stubbornly enmeshed in every fiber of the fabric of life.

I like to think that what Soeur St. Cybard did, not only saved me, but endowed me with a rare example of great goodness. The force of that example has persisted into the present. It lives in the handful of rescuers, the few righteous Gentiles who risked everything to save Jews and other fugitives from the Nazis, from the Holocaust.

These examples of "light piercing the darkness," beacons of morality, anchors of goodness... are something to grasp when nothing else holds.

Finally, Soeur St. Cybard, I have also written this story for you.

**Mademoiselle Guinêt and Josie on the school steps – July, 1999
Mademoiselle was instrumental in arranging the reunion in
Lesterps, October 2000, at which I was made "Premiere
Citoyenne."**

Josie standing before the entrance of the school. Note that it is the same porch where she stood on the stairs in the cover picture.

The dreaded enclosure. By 1999, the little tree was gone. The building had long ceased being used. The yard was overgrown.

The Lévy family lived in the two downstairs corner rooms in Montbron. Josie and cousin Robert Lévy, now 75 years old, lives in Metz, France

Mademoiselle Guinet & Josie walking up the street from the school – October, 2000.

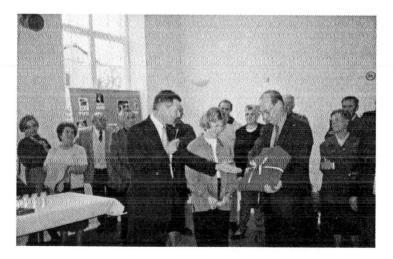

Daniel Soupizet, mayor of Lesterps, presenting the Coat of Arms of the town to Josie at a ceremony declaring her Premiere Citoyenne Honoraire of this 1000 year old village.

Josie Levy Martin

Tree planting outside the present primary school.

Les anciennes élèves de l'école catholique de Lesterps ont retrouvé et fêté Josie.

**The former students of the school gathered together to honor
the hidden child who is very moved –
Lesterps, October, 2000.**

ABOUT THE AUTHOR

Josie Martin was born in France shortly before World War II. She came to the U.S. in 1947. She began almost 50 years later to write of the hidden child she had been, to acknowledge the life of a small girl, to pay homage to the remarkable Soeur St. Cybard, and to remember the many righteous acts of ordinary people that allowed her to survive the darkest of times.

Ms. Martin is a writer and a school psychologist. She writes a column on children in school settings for the Larchmont Chronicle. Her work has also appeared in The Los Angeles Times, Parent's Magazine, and The Jewish Journal.

She finally returned to the village of Lesterps in October of 2000 to be declared its "First Honorary Citizen" in a ceremony. The nun had died long before in 1968. Ms. Martin is married and has one son. She lives in Los Angeles.

Printed in the United States
16168LVS00003B/253-417